I USED TO HATE THE ACT TOO.

How to Conquer the #1 College Admissions Test.

Andre Kiss, founder of testpreplive.com

Copyright © 2015 by Andre Kiss
All rights reserved.

www.testpreplive.com

Cover Art: Kailey Goodnuff
Back Cover Photo: Adam Atkinson

Book Illustrations by: Kailey Goodnuff and Samantha Soffera

The ACT® is a registered trademark of ACT, Inc.

The author, book, and any written content or images are in no way affiliated with or sponsored by ACT, Inc.

ISBN-13: 978-1511855693

TABLE OF CONTENTS

Preface: *My journey*

PART 1: THE FUNDAMENTALS

Chapter One: *Prepare your mind*

1.1. Success Does Not Happen Overnight
1.2. Get Rid of the Gremlin
1.3. Three Things to Remember
1.4. Motivation Sheet

Chapter Two: *Hacking your physiology*

2.1. What You Nom On Matters
2.2. Sleep to Learn. Learn to Sleep.
2.3. Study Intelligently

Chapter Three: *Pacing*

PART 2: THE STRATEGIES

3.99 Two Strategies for Every Section

Chapter Four: *The English Test*

4.1 Subject-Verb Agreement.
4.2 Short and Sweet
4.3 Don't be Redundant
4.4 Odd One Out
4.5 The Semicolon Test
4.6 Tenses
4.7 It's Irrelevant

4.8 Maintain Parallel Structure
4.9 Who Loves Commas?
4.10 Summarize
4.11 Active and Passive Voice
4.12 One vs. You
4.13 The Three i-t-s
4.14 Might've, Could've, Would've

4.15 Two General English Section Strategies

Chapter Five: *The Math Test*

5.1 Never Work in Fractions
5.2 The Distance Formula
5.3 Average (Also Known as the Arithmetic Mean)
5.4 Combinations
5.5 Get Concrete
5.6 Percents
5.7 Plug n' Chug
5.8 Slope
5.9 Master y=mx+b
5.10 Exponents
5.11 Logs: Exponents that got fancy
5.12 Function
5.13 Angles and Angle-Algebra
5.14 Triangles
5.15 Circle
5.16 The Circle Equation
5.17 SOH-CAH-TOA
5.18 Other Trigonometry

Chapter Six: *The Reading Test*

6.1 Come Up With an Answer in Your Head
6.2 Get Context
6.3 Underline Keywords
6.4 Check Every Part of the Answer
6.5 ACT Test Writers Are Politically Correct

Chapter Seven: *The Science Test*

7.1 The Three Types of Science Section Passages
7.2 Don't Read (For the Most Part…)
7.3 Become Acquainted
7.4 It's All About Relationships
7.5 What's a Variable?

Chapter Eight: *The Essay*

8.1 The 6 Simple Ways You Will Conquer the Essay
8.2 An Exceptional Essay Embodying the 6 Principles

Chapter Nine: *The Week of the Test*

Answers to Practice Problems

ACKNOWLEDGEMENTS

There are too many wonderful people who have helped me in completing this project. I will do my best to name a few.

Mom, Dad, Will, Nicole:
You have all been an awesome support system that has helped get through this process from its inception to its completion. I love you all very much.

Kailey and Sam:
This book wouldn't be the same without your awesome, wacky drawings. You guys rock.

Julia (my Frenchie) :
I never cease to be impressed with your knowledge of the English language. Your edits were a huge help.

Armen:
For continually keeping me motivated and inspiring me with your vision! You played a larger role than you know.

To those who believed in me:
You gave me the motivation I needed to continue forging ahead when things got rough.

To those who didn't believe in me:
You gave me the motivation I needed to continue forging ahead when things got rough.

And finally, I'd like to dedicate this book to *Monica*:

You are the greatest light in my universe and I thank god every day for bringing you into my life.

ABOUT THE ILLUSTRATORS

Kailey Goodnuff is an artist and illustrator from Easton, PA. Kailey's work deals with issues such as mental health, identity, politics, and personality in order to expose what is below the surface. She enjoys making art meant to be viewed as nonsensical to remind herself to enjoy life and not take everything too seriously.

Samantha Soffera is an artist from Easton, PA. While currently a sophomore at Easton Area High School, she intends to pursue degrees in both Early Childhood Education and Art after graduating. She is a lover of art, music, food, and fashion.

PREFACE
My Journey

"A journey of a thousand miles begins with a single step"

—Lao-tzu

When I tell people I'm a test prep tutor, I tend to get a few different reactions. Perhaps the most common, though, is the simultaneously bewildered and pitying "God bless you for subjecting yourself to such torture on a daily basis!" reaction. "I could never do that, but I sure wish I had you when I took the test," they say. To their surprise, my response to them is, "I wish I had me too."

Like most people I encounter, I absolutely detested the ACT's back in high school; the test gave me a lot of anxiety. I was always told I was smart and I identified myself as someone who was good at math, but the thought of not doing well on the test terrified me.

What would the other kids at school think of me? What would my parents think of me? Worst of all, what would I think of me? What if I'm not as smart as I thought I was?

At the end of the day, though, I had to suck it up and see how the cookie would crumble.

Because my family didn't have enough money for a tutor, my preparation consisted of my mom dropping me off at Barnes and Noble and sitting at the cafe for three hours at a time with my blank notebook completing practice tests from the prep books they had in stock. Finally, I took the test and after the longest three weeks of my life, I received my results.

I missed the mark. While my scores were good, there weren't the scores I had hoped for. Regardless, I still got into a great school, learned a lot, had great experiences, and graduated at the top of my class. This should be the first clue in this book that not getting your ideal test scores does not mean the end of the world.

After graduating college, I started working as a test prep tutor. After working with hundreds of students, I started to recognize something: there were only so many different types of questions on the ACT. If a student just studied these and knew these question types inside and out they could improve their score significantly. The content was just the first piece of the puzzle, however. Something else was missing: my students had no idea how to prepare their psychology and physiology. Things such as efficient study habits, the importance of nutrition and sleep, and writing down their goals, despite their importance, were never taught to students!

As soon as I began to implement these principles with my students, I began to see the results. While before the a student might have increased their composite score by two or three points, now it could be as much as five or even six in some cases!

I have coached hundreds of students across the United States, Europe, and South America to success on the ACT, and I take the both the ACT and the SAT at least once a year to keep my skills sharp. Empowering students to reach their true potential is the most rewarding thing in the world for me.

My goal with this book is to offer anyone the guidance that I wish I had when I took the test. I will provide you with all of the tools you will need to achieve your greatest possible score, but is up to you to put the tools into practice to see definite results. If you adopt the strategies and methods in this book, not only will you dominate the test, but you'll also find yourself excelling in other areas of your life

If your car breaks down on the highway, it's probably not in your best interest to be traveling with a friend who has never had car troubles. You will want to be with someone who has had to change a tire or replace a fuse, because experience has given them the knowledge they need to fix the problem. While I am not a savant who effortlessly got perfect scores on his standardized tests the first time around, I am someone who has learned the right ways and the wrong ways to achieve success on the ACT and I am here to help coach you to your true potential.

How to Use This Book Best

I've broken up the book into two parts. Part 1 is entitled "The Fundamentals", while Part 2 covers "The Strategies."

Part 1 contains the fundamentals you need to master in order to most effectively apply the strategies in the next part. Part 2 contains the section-specific strategies and information that will get you through virtually any question the test can and will throw at you.

While the first part of the book doesn't cover any specific section-based strategies, I truly believe it's the most important part. This section is where you'll learn the mental and physiological fundamentals that will set you up for success not only on the ACT, but in any endeavor in your life. How you eat, sleep, and study is terribly crucial to succeeding on the ACT. You can know every concept and every strategy there is, but if you sit down on test day and your mind and body are not in peak condition, you are simply not going to do your best.

Whether you continue to implement these principles in your life after the test is up to you, but while preparing for the test itself you should be following them as closely as possible. I have a feeling, though, that once you see how easy your life can be, mentally, physiologically, etc., you won't consider going back to your old ways.

No other test-prep tutor or company I have ever come across emphasizes psychology, diet, sleep, or learning strategies for test prep, and this is precisely why the methodology in this book will set you apart from the pack.

Timing Your Prep

The time you have until your test date may also influence how you use this book.

Ideally, test prep should begin four to eight weeks before the test to make sure there is ample time to effectively absorb new strategies and eliminate old habits. This, however, is flexible depending on the individual. For those who have four to eight weeks before the test, you should read this book in order from front to back cover.

For those of you pressed for time, read what you can from the chapters and review the summaries after each strategy. However, make sure you don't skip the section on pacing, which is crucial.

Four Things You Will Need to Use This Book Successfully

1. **The Real ACT Guide**

    While this book is filled with incredibly effective strategies and techniques, it is meant to work in conjunction with The Real ACT Prep Guide, *Peterson's; 3 edition (September 6, 2011)* (RACT).

    Since RACT is written by the same people who make the ACT, the problems on the five practice tests inside of it are authentic, not written by some guy in Bangalore, India, who was paid seven dollars an hour to come up with questions that were "similar enough." I use this book with all of my clients, and students who are improving your score would buy RACT anyway.

    Furthermore, in addition to the practice problems I wrote at the end of most strategies, I also listed problems of each type in RACT with the test number, page number, and question number so that you can see exactly how a certain question type appears on the tests. All of this is intended to give you a greater mastery of the material to leave you feeling like a champ on test day.

2. **Perseverance and Determination**

    This one speaks for itself. Nothing worth having comes easy and you are going to have to work hard to improve your score.

    There will be times when you are tired, times when you might not feel like finishing your practice test, times when you're don't feel like reviewing strategies. That is all normal. But whenever you feel like skipping your work or cutting corners, I want you to ask yourself the following question:

"If I don't do what I'm supposed to right now, will it help me or hurt me in the future?"

The answer you give yourself to this question will take care of your decision.

3. **Humility: Leave Your Ego at the Door**

   Bad habits die hard.

   A large part of becoming a more successful ACT-taker is breaking your old and inefficient habits and replacing them with the new ones I offer here. You may find some of the information and strategies silly; you will probably feel uncomfortable using them at first. But this is exactly what you need to generate great results! Remember, if you do what you've always done, you will get what you've always gotten.

   Albert Einstein once said, "The definition of insanity is doing the same thing over and over while expecting different results." Don't be that student who desperately holds on to her old ways. Following these strategies as closely as possible is essential for improving your score. Trust the tutor!

4. **Scrap Paper**

   If you look at the practice problems in the English and Math sections, you'll notice that there isn't sufficient space to solve the problem by writing the work in the book. This was intentional.

   The idea wasn't motivated by the desire to save trees (although that's important too), but rather by the desire for you to learn better.

   As you'll see later on, learning is simply a matter of repetition. If I had left ample space after the problems, you would only be able to fill out the problems once. At a later date, it would be difficult to review the problem because all of your work would already be in front of you. Erasing all your work would be a nuisance and would likely still leave pencil markings.

By using scrap paper for the practice problems, you're able to repeat the problem as many times as you need to in order to truly learn the information.

Part 1
The Fundamentals

CHAPTER 1
Prepare Your Mind

"I've missed more than 9000 shots in my career. I've lost almost 300 games. 26 times, I've been trusted to take the game-winning shot and missed. I've failed over and over and over again in my life. And that is why I succeed."

— Michael Jordan

The year was 1996 and an unemployed writer had just received the dreaded call from her agent. "They shot it back," her agent said, uncomfortable to be the bearer of bad news yet once more. "Again?" the author thought to herself.

This was the 11th publisher she had sent her manuscript to, and, just like all the others, it rejected her work using the same justification she had heard 10 times before: "Children's books don't turn a profit."

Ironically the 12th publishing house to which she sent her manuscript loved it, published it, and helped make it a smashing success, transforming her from a single mother struggling to make ends meet into one of the wealthiest and most well-known individuals in the world. Today, her books have collectively sold over 500 million copies worldwide and been translated to over 70 different languages.

Just who was this surprising success story? None other than J.K. Rowling, author of the Harry Potter series.

Success Does Not Happen Overnight

People tend to look at an individual and only see the fruits of the person's success, overlooking the overwhelming effort it took to get them there. They see the convertible sports car, the name in the paper, and the best-selling book, but they don't see the countless hours spent in solitude, the long caffeinated nights, or the waste-paper basket filled with crumpled-up ideas before the right one finally came along.

That's right, boys and girls. Success does not happen overnight*.

- Fired by a newspaper editor who described him as someone who lacked imagination and had no good ideas, Walt Disney, needless to say, went on to prove him wrong.

- When starting his first company, now multibillionaire and owner of the Dallas Mavericks, Mark Cuban, routinely stayed up until two in the morning working on his business, and even went seven years without a vacation.

- Michael Jordan didn't make the varsity basketball team in high school. But did that stop him? Did the 6-time NBA all-star, and all-time leader in scoring on the Chicago Bulls, let this obstacle keep him from greatness? If it had, we wouldn't be talking about him today.

*A site I really enjoyed visiting to reinforce this fact was
"http://www.literaryrejections.com/best-sellers-initially-rejected/"
(accessed on February 20th, 2015.)

I don't claim to have any magical secrets to instantaneously improve your ACT score. Magical shortcuts to success are about as real as Unicorn Vampires with great calves.

I hope you didn't plan to sleep tonight...

As any successful person will tell you, accomplishing any difficult task requires time and hard work. My goal with you is to take the guesswork out of getting a good test score and to show you the road you need to take to do your best. I will provide you with the tools you will need to succeed, but if you don't practice them or study consistently, you won't reach your true potential.

The point here is, in any aspect of your life, especially test prep, great accomplishments require proper planning and hard work. Many times it's not easy. Reaching your target score of a 24, 31, or 36 is absolutely feasible, but it won't happen without some effort.

Get Rid of the Gremlin

In each of us there is a little gremlin who lives in our heads and comes out from time to time introduce doubt and negativity into our lives. It likes to bring us down. Rather than empower us to help us achieve our ultimate potential, it loves to tell us how incompetent, silly, or worthless we are—how there is no point in trying because we are going to fail anyway. While every individual does this to varying degrees, we all have a tendency to doubt ourselves or fear failure at some point in our lives.

The gremlin loves to introduce doubt and negativity into your life.

Life is hard when you are your own worst enemy. When we fixate on the negatives and beat ourselves up over little mistakes, we create mental barriers that keep us from achieving our best.

In my life, I had a lot of limiting beliefs about my abilities as a writer and an entrepreneur. Just two years ago, If you had asked me I would ever write a book or start my own business I probably would have laughed at you.

One book and two businesses later, I know I obviously wasn't lacking the capacity of accomplishing these things, but it was my previously established negative beliefs about who I was that limited me from doing my best. As we move forward from this section, I want you reflect on what self-limiting beliefs you might have about your performance on the ACT.

Keeping all of this in mind, let's discuss four important things as you prepare for this test and even after you move on from test prep.

Four Important Things for Prep and for Life

1. You Are Human and You Are Going to Make Mistakes.

Life is not about achieving and maintaining perfection. It is about making progress. The ACT is just the same. Setting unrealistic expectations of yourself will lead to a lot of pain and disappointment, and cause you to lose motivation very quickly.

Don't expect to get perfect scores on every section from the beginning. However, if you study diligently, you should expect to see incremental improvement in your scores over time. How large or small that improvement is depends entirely on your effort.

2. Make Those Mistakes, but Learn From Them.

So now that you've accepted that you will make mistakes, what do we do with that?

It's not the events in our lives that matter, but rather how we interpret those events. Will you see your struggles and your weak areas on the ACT with a glass-half-full or a glass-half-empty perspective?

It's the difference between saying *"I got all the geometry problems wrong in the math section! I'm hopeless!"* and, *"I got all the geometry problems wrong in the math section! Now that I have this information, I can work harder to improve my geometry knowledge and boost my score."*

Do you see the difference between these perspectives? Only one of them is actually helpful for us. The other is just wasteful.

In life there is no such thing as failure. There are only results. What separates average individuals from superior individuals is that the latter makes the choice to learn from their results.

Don't dwell on your mistakes. Observe them and learn from them.

3. Believe That You Can

> *"Whether you think you can, or you think you can't– you're right."*
> HENRY FORD

This quote beautifully captures the idea of the self-fulfilling prophecies we create that hold us back.

Do you believe you are capable of improving?
Do you believe you are intelligent enough to increase your score?
Do you believe you are good enough to get into your dream college?

These are all questions that you need to ask yourself, but answering "yes" to them is not enough. You have to truly believe it.

When we put labels on who we are, on our identity, we will always act in ways that are consistent with those labels.

So if you don't believe you're capable of improving, why would you ever take the steps necessary in order to actually improve? If you don't believe you're good enough to get into your dream college, why would you take the actions necessary to do so?

Do not misunderstand me: belief is not the same as false confidence. If you show up on test day without any preparation, just believing you're going to get a great score without trying, you're going to have a pretty big wake-up call when you receive your scores. Prior preparation is important for success, but in order to tap 100 percent of ourselves we need to truly believe we are capable and visualize ourselves achieving our goal.

4. Define Your Goals

It's impossible to know if you are on the right track to success if you don't know what it is you are aiming for. Consider the following questions:

What schools are you trying to get into?

What scores do these schools have listed on their website?

Why is it important to you to better your test scores?

There is a blank sheet on the next page with these questions written on it. I want you to write your answers to these questions, rip out the page, and hang it up in a visible place in your room, somewhere you will see it every day.

The overwhelming majority of students I work with have the same unenthusiastic, skeptical initial reaction to this exercise: "This is lame. Why do I need to do this? How is this going to help me?"

The truth is, the more you interact with this paper, the more you'll have your goals on the forefront of your mind. The more you have your goals on the forefront of your mind, the more likely you will be to do what it takes to achieve them and the harder it will be to quit.

If you're unwilling to even write these down, chances are you might be unconsciously trying to sabotage yourself. Think about it: deep down you know that if you hung up the paper and then decided to quit, you would have some "stupid" paper reminding you of your failure!

Fill out the following sheet, hang it up somewhere where you will see it and interact with it often, and see how powerfully it can help you achieve those goals.

(Rip me out and hang out and hang me on your wall!)

ACT MOTIVATION SHEET

"Failure will never overtake me if my determination to succeed is strong enough."

MY TOP SCHOOLS	SCORE RANGES

BASELINE SCORES (*scores from a diagnostic or previous test*)

ENGLISH   MATH   READING   SCIENCE   ESSAY

I, _____ , am willing to do everything it takes to improve my ACT score, because I recognize the importance of preparing intelligently for my college application process and my future. Although I know at times I might be tempted to throw in the towel and watch hours upon hours of the internet's finest cat videos instead, I will not give up at the first sign of difficulty and will study tediously for (what is hopefully) 4-8 weeks before my test date.

Signed _____

On _____ , _____, 20_____

I Used to Hate the ACT, too. - Andre Kiss, *founder of* testpreplive.com   1.4

CHAPTER 1 SUMMARY

- Those who succeed are often the ones who work the hardest. Are you willing to put in the hard work to improve your score?

- You are a human, not a robot. Instead of placing unrealistic demands of perfection upon yourself, recognize that the goal you should be aiming for is week-to-week improvement.

- Interacting with your goal sheet with your ideal scores and top schools will help you take the action necessary to achieve them.

CHAPTER 2
Hacking Your Physiology

"The higher your energy level, the more efficient your body, the more efficient your body, the better you feel and the more you will use your talent to produce outstanding results."

— Tony Robbins

How do you feel when you wake up in the morning? Do you set your alarm for 30 minutes earlier than you need to because you subconsciously know that you will spend the first half-hour of the morning squirming in your sheets, moaning like a zombie? Or do you open your eyes and immediately plant your feet on the ground, ready to take on the day and all of its challenges?

Which do you feel like when you wake up in the morning?

Unfortunately, most people belong to the first category. It's easy to fall into the trap of staying up until the wee hours of the morning, mindlessly surfing the web watching cat videos, and scrolling through pages upon pages of social media. It's just as easy to eat only nutritionally-empty food that tastes good. Unfortunately, these lifestyle choices leave these individuals lethargic and lacking energy, many of whom rely on caffeine for a pick-me-up. What is even more unfortunate, though, is that they don't believe they can escape this vicious cycle of fatigue.

But what creates the difference between those individuals who triumphantly climb Mount Everest and those who sheepishly struggle to climb back on the couch after falling off it? To answer that question, we have to look at human physiology. The human potential is truly infinite and if we prepare ourselves beginning with our physiology, we will quickly see that anything is possible.

"Why is any of this relevant?"

The ACT is a test of endurance and stamina (it's a little less than 4 hours). To be on our A-game for every second of that test we have to start with a strong physiology. If we sleep right and nourish ourselves properly, we will be prepared with greater energy, concentration, and mental resilience for the test.

Additionally, I am going to let you in on the science of learning and how you can use this knowledge to learn anything quicker and better. This will help you excel in your high school classes and is something you should carry with you into college.

This all sounds pretty simple, right? It absolutely is. But unfortunately, no test prep company I have come across ever covers these topics crucial for success.

This section is about setting yourself up for success from our very core. If we have a strong core, everything else will easily fall into place. If we don't, of course the opposite is true. When we have an abundance of energy with which to deal with the unpredictability of life's problems, life becomes exponentially easier. This knowledge will help you get to that state if you aren't already there.

If you've always wanted to have in-your-face *"no-I'm-not-on-drugs-just-excited"* energy, there's no reason why you can't. You just have to implement the following principles.

1. Learn to Sleep, Sleep to Learn

What do birds, dogs, humans, and platypuses have in common? They all sleep, of course. Even creatures without brains, such as plants and microorganisms, have states of inactivity which closely resemble human sleep. There are many theories about why we sleep, but one thing that most neuroscientists agree on is that we sleep to learn.eee

REM Sleep is Crucial for Learning

To an outside observer, someone sleeping may seem pretty inactive, but the reality could not be farther from the truth. As you sleep, your brain is carrying out all kinds of important processes, sorting through the experiences and information you went through the day before.

By looking at a graph of brain waves, we see the brain fluctuates between five different stages of activity over the course of the night: Stage 1, Stage 2, Stage 3, Stage 4, and Rapid Eye Movement (REM) sleep.

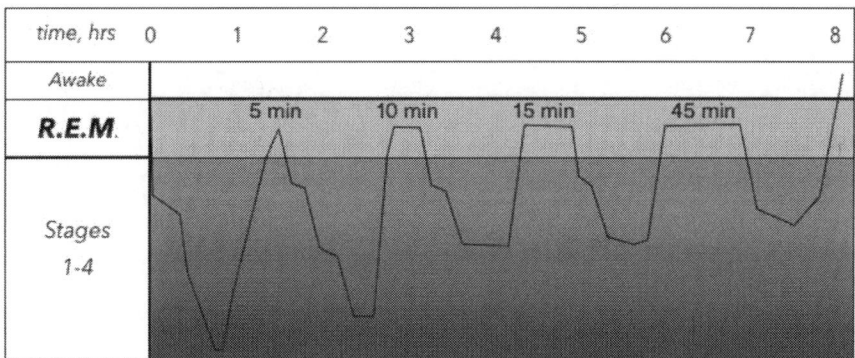

The longer you are asleep, the longer your brain stays in REM each time it reaches it. More REM = More Learning

The most important stage here for our purposes is REM, which stimulates brain regions important for *learning and memory.*

The longer you are asleep, the longer your brain stays in REM each time it reaches it. The first time your brain enters REM it stays there for only five minutes, but during the last cycle, it can get up to a full hour of REM! This is why it's so important that you get between seven to eight hours of sleep a night. Skip those last two hours and you could miss out on more than one half of your possible REM sleep, making it harder for you to learn or remember anything.

Circadian Rhythms: Our Bodies' Timekeepers

The biological processes in our bodies operate on their own special schedule: these are called circadian rhythms. The more stable these rhythms are, the more efficiently they will perform.

What happens when we go to bed one night at 2 AM and sleep eight hours, and the next night go to bed at 10 PM and sleep eight hours as well? Even though you slept the same amount, you will feel groggy the next day. With sleep it's not just about **quantity: quality** is just as important. So keep in mind that after making a major change in your sleep schedule, it takes three to four days for your rhythms to reset.

The better we can stick to a regular sleep schedule, the more efficiently our circadian rhythms flow, the more energy we will have, and the more focus we can dedicate to studying for the test.

Never Pull All-Nighters

As heroic as it might seem to stay up all night studying for a test you have in the morning, it simply doesn't work.

Because you will be cutting your sleep short, not only will you be getting less REM sleep which means you won't consolidate the information as well, but you will also be less alert and focused in general.

2. What You Nom on Matters

Too many people today think proper diet is all about having a great beach body, but not many understand the importance of proper nutrition for living a healthy and productive lifestyle—especially a lifestyle in which you have an abundance of energy.

If you eat a Pop-Tart your body is going to respond differently than it would if you ate a carrot. We've all experienced this before. What happens when you eat a whole bag of jelly beans all at once? I think we all know that experience! The sugar rush in the first 20-30 minutes is great, and then you crash and just want to pass out. But why?

Someone's about to crash.

Blood Sugar and Energy

Every time you eat your food is broken down into glucose (a natural sugar) which enters your bloodstream and triggers an insulin response, which helps the body use this sugar. However, depending on what kind of food you eat, the insulin response affects your body quite differently.

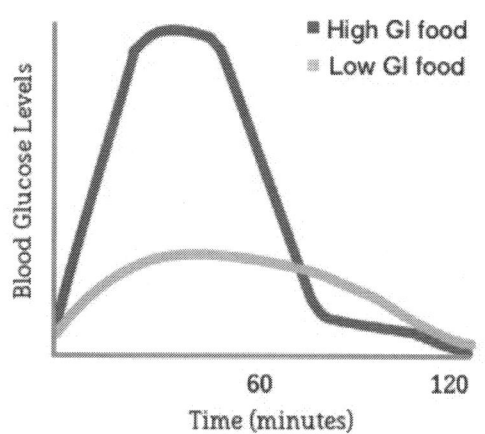

When your blood sugar crashes, it's bad news bears for your focus and concentration.

Eating processed or refined foods, such as white bread, cookies, or anything with high-fructose corn syrup, will produce an excess of insulin, which makes the body burn through the glucose (energy) too quickly. This will put you into a state of lethargy, fatigue, and irritability, something not helpful for studying, learning, or focusing.

Eating natural whole foods, including beans, most fruits and vegetables, and nuts, will provide you with long-lasting sustainable energy. This will not only improve your mood but also your concentration. It almost sounds too good to be true, right?!

The following is a list of foods that will keep your energy stable and keep you from crashing throughout the course of the day. The more you are able to incorporate these into your diet, the better you will feel. And even if you are not able to eat these every day, you should, at the very least, eat them the day before and the day of the test.

Low GI foods	High GI foods
Whole Wheat or Pumpernickel Bread	White Bread
Poultry or Fish	White Rice
Pasta	Instant Mac n' cheese
Eggs	Pancakes
Steel-Cut Oatmeal	Most Breakfast Cereals; Oatmeal Packets
Most Fruits and Vegetables	Chips
Nuts and Seeds	Cookies
Greek Yogurt	Fruit juices
Almond Milk (un- or lightly sweetened)	Soda
Beans	Most Desserts

Foods to eat and avoid for stable energy levels and strong concentration

Avoid Large Meals

You may have heard the popular myth that the reason why you get sleepy after Thanksgiving Day dinner is due to an amino acid in the turkey, tryptophan, which is also responsible for regulating sleep in humans.

While it is true that turkey meat does contain some tryptophan, it doesn't contain nearly enough to make you sleepy. The real culprit here is just the sheer amount of deliciousness we stuff our faces with.

When we eat huge meals, the stomach needs to work harder to digest the food, and therefore sends more blood to the digestive system, taking away blood from other parts of the body responsible for alertness and activity, like the brain.

Moral of the story: don't eat large meals right before you need to sit down and study or take a practice test.

3. Study Intelligently

If you haven't picked up on it yet, one of the biggest themes in this book is efficiency. Doing anything in life one way when there's a better and faster way is simply a waste of time. And with learning, just as with anything else, there is an efficient and inefficient way to do it.

For the sake of making my point, let's imagine we have two twins named Eustace and Gretchen—typical names, right?

Since they are identical twins, Eustace and Gretchen have the same genes, the same brain, and the same ability—*they are equal in almost every regard.*

Both ambitious violinists, they are each auditioning for the position of lead violinist in the city orchestra, in which they will have to perform Jay-Z's inspiring classic, "99

Problems". However, while they both practice seven hours a week, they have different practice schedules.

Gretchen practices every day of the week for one hour each day.

Eustace only practices on Sundays for 7 hours.

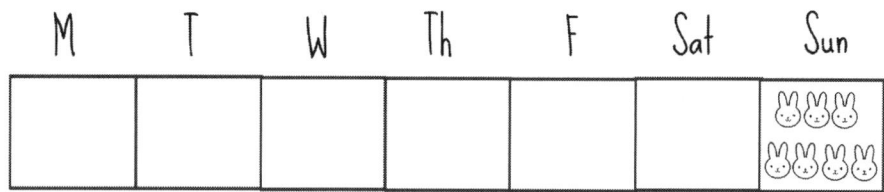

Even though they have the same brain, same ability, and practiced for the same amount of time, who do you think is going to know the music better, make the least amount of mistakes, and get the part?

If you answered Gretchen, you are right on the money.

While you may not know exactly why you intuitively chose Gretchen, you still felt pretty confident about your answer, right? The reason for the difference in performance comes down to simple neuroscience.

The Neuroscience of Learning

To give you a brief neuroscience lesson, the brain learns by strengthening and rewiring the connections between its tiniest components, neurons. Another way to think about your brain is like a muscle. The more you exercise a skill or a memory, the stronger, or more efficient those neural connections become. So, when you learn something, whether it be riding a unicycle or getting better at running from the law in *Grand Theft Auto*, you are actually changing your brain on a molecular level!

Your brain learns best when you work it out consistently.

The brain does this strengthening and rewiring best when active learning happens consistently. This means you will actually learn information better if you study one hour a day for a week, instead of studying seven hours for one day a week.

Because your brain can only do so much in a day, instead of intensely studying for one or two days per week, make sure you complete practice tests consistently throughout the week over three to four days, while spending 20 minutes each day to review strategies.

Your brain can only do so much each day.

Your brain is just like any other muscle in your body. If you wanted to get in amazing shape you wouldn't go to the gym once a week for eight hours. That would be silly! To see real results, you would go to the gym three to four times a week and workout one to two hours per day.

Do your best to study consistently throughout the week.

While in the beginning of prep a good rule of thumb is to complete one section per day. Once you are one and a half to two weeks from test day taking full practice tests in one sitting can help you prepare your mind for the stamina needed for the test.

Sun	Mon	Tues	Wed	Thurs	Fri	Sat
MATH		READING	SCIENCE		ENGLISH	ESSAY

How you should be studying in the first several weeks of prep

CHAPTER 2 SUMMARY

To be on our A-game for the test, and even for life in general, we have to make sure we properly rest and nourish our bodies.

Sleep

- Your brain needs REM sleep for learning and memory.

- Get 7-8 hours of shut-eye per night for maximal REM sleep.

- Go to bed and wake up within a half-hour of the same time every day to maximize the efficiency of your circadian rhythms.

- All-nighters are incredibly inefficient and should be avoided like the plague, especially the night before a test.

Diet

- Foods with a high Glycemic Index will spike your blood sugar, give you a temporary boost and then leave you feeling like Jabba the Hutt.

- Big meals and fatty foods are hard to digest and will also drain you of energy.

- Foods with low Glycemic Index will keep your blood sugar stable and leave you with energy to do things, including dominating the test.

Studying

- Learning is simply the brain's process of strengthening and re-wiring its neurons.

- This strengthening and rewiring happens best when you study or practice something consistently over time.

- In the beginning of your prep, aim to finish a practice three to four days per week while reviewing relevant concepts and strategies for 20 minutes every day of the week.

- During the last one and a half to two weeks of prep, complete one to two practice tests per week, while reviewing concepts and strategies for 15 minutes every day of the week.

CHAPTER 3
Pace Yourself

One of the biggest things ACT-takers struggle with is pacing. It is tough to know exactly how quickly or slowly to work through a section, especially if you haven't practiced it before. To make things even more difficult, almost every section has a different rhythm to master.

In the English section, you have a question every 36 seconds.
In the Math section, you have roughly one minute per question.
In the Reading and Science sections, you have about 53 seconds per question.

Order	Test	Time	?'s	Sec/question
1	English	45 minutes	75	36
2	Math	60 minutes	60	60
3	Reading	35 minutes	40	53
4	Science	35 minutes	40	53

Test breakdown, not including the essay

Aside from learning and practicing the subject-specific strategies, the tips below will help tighten up your pacing game.

Get a Sports Watch!

You should buy a sports watch with a chronometer function to time yourself during practice tests, so that on test day, you have no doubts about how much time has passed or how much time you have left. It is a simple 20 dollar investment that can make a huge difference. There are two simple reasons for this.

Reason #1: You Can't Rely on the Clock in the Classroom.

The clock could be completely broken.

It could mark time too fast or too slowly.

The view of the clock could be blocked by the girl with the humongous head in front of you.

The clock could be behind you. Do you really want to have to turn all the way around every three minutes?

Lastly, there could be no clock in the room.

These are the pitfalls of relying on the clock in the classroom to time yourself through the test. Using your own stopwatch will eliminate them.

Reason #2: You Definitely Can't Rely on the Proctor.

I had a student once who showed up to take the ACT with a lot of confidence. We had been working together for the past six weeks and she was doing quite well, scoring in the 30s on almost every section.

Despite my advice to use a sports watch to time herself, she decided to take the test without it.

The test began and students started on the English section. However, just 20 minutes into the 45-minute English section, the utterly clueless proctor stated "Five minutes left." Realizing they had more than half of the questions to answer and such a short time left, the students panicked and started frantically filling in answers.

Several minutes later, the proctor caught his mistake and informed the students they actually had another 20 minutes left. Imagine the chaos! Most students had already filled in their answer sheet, and now had to go back, erase their answers, and carry on like nothing had happened!

The panic and stress from this incident depleted the confidence that the student had built up, and threw her off her A-game for the rest of the test. Even though she had been consistently scoring in the 30s in the timed practice tests leading up to test-day, she scored in the mid-20s in nearly every section that day— *a huge price to pay for not using her sports watch.*

Take Timed Practice Tests

One of the best things you can do to tighten up your pacing is to take several timed practice tests (using your sports watch, of course) before the test date.

When beginning your prep, I don't recommend taking whole tests in one sitting. At first, it's better to finish a timed section every day or every other day while also studying and reviewing the strategies in this book. However, as you approach your test date you should be taking more sections together, having taken several full practice tests in one sitting before the test. This is usually easiest for students to fit in on a Saturday or Sunday morning.

Whether you're completing full tests or just sections, it's crucial you always simulate the conditions you'll encounter on test day to the best of your ability. This means you need to make sure you're abiding by the following rules:

HOW TO SIMULATE TEST DAY CONDITIONS

- Find a quiet space where you won't be interrupted or distracted by your dog, your best friend Tina, your Aunt Gertrude and her delicious apple pie, or anything or anyone else.

- Turn your cell phone off or on silent. I assure you Twitter will still be there after your Math Section.

- Use your sports watch to time yourself.

- Don't give yourself any extra time.

Pacing: *In Summary...*

- Don't rely on the clock; get a sports watch with a chronometer function to time yourself while taking the tests.

- This will help your brain get accustomed to the pacing and help eliminate risk from things out of your control like unreliable and poorly placed clocks, or irresponsible proctors.

How to Simulate Test Day Conditions

- Find a quiet space where you won't be interrupted or distracted.

- Turn your cell phone off or on silent.

- Use your sports watch to time yourself.

- Do not give yourself any extra time.

Part 2
The Strategies

Two Strategies for Every Section

Before we go into the nuances of each specific section, there are a couple of strategies that are crucial for you to practice on every section of the test. From English to Science, these are equally important for each section. While they may seem simplistic, if you implement these two simple strategies, your score will improve.

1. Don't Get Hung up on Questions

You shouldn't spend more than a minute on most ACT questions.

One of the biggest mistakes students make is spending too much time on a question. Look at a question, and do your best to solve it. If you are absolutely 100 percent clueless about how to solve it, or if you've spent a minute on it and don't feel close to the solution, *draw a circle around the problem in the test booklet and come back to it after you've been through the whole section.*

You want to economize your time and make sure you are able to see as many questions that you know how to solve as possible to maximize your score. Sometimes, coming back to a problem with a refreshed mind can allow us to see the solution.

2. Cross S*%# out.

Stuff. Cross stuff out.

This is a simple strategy, but one that can gain you valuable minutes and points on the test.

When you look at a question, we need to methodically evaluate every answer and immediately cross out the ones we know are wrong.

There are two reasons for this…

Reason #1: Re-evaluating Answers Wastes Time

Consider the following question:

31. If a magic genie could grant you one wish of your choice, what would it be?

   A. A glass of lemonade
   B. A DVD copy of *One Direction: Live in Concert*
   C. A breath mint
   D. To become fluent in every language
   E. To become a prodigy at every musical instrument

Now, unless you are crazy about lemonade, adore boy bands, or just ate some garlic knots, chances are you are going to be torn between D and E. But it is a hard call to make.

Let's say you are able to cross out three of the answer choices, but you are unsure about the last two, so you circle the question and move on. Once you reach the end of the section and go back to the circled question, you won't have to re-evaluate the three answer choices you had already crossed out. You will immediately know they are wrong and you can focus on the potentially correct answers instead. This will save you valuable seconds that can add up to minutes when you have multiple circled questions in a section. I can't emphasize enough how important this is!

Reason #2: Visual Focus is Key

So let's say again, you have narrowed it down to answer choices D and E. Now you need to focus hard to make sure you answer correctly. Let me ask you this: in which of the following pictures is it easier to focus on answer choices D and E?

This one?

A. A glass of lemonade

B. A DVD copy of *One Direction: Live in concert*

C. A breath mint

D. To become fluent in every language

E. To become a prodigy at every musical instrument

…or this one?

~~A. A glass of lemonade~~

~~B. A DVD copy of *One Direction: Live in concert*~~

~~C. A breath mint~~

D. To become fluent in every language

E. To become a prodigy at every musical instrument

Without a doubt, the crossed out answer choices in the second one make it easier for us to focus on D and E. Even though in your mind you know that the first three answer choices are incorrect, your attention is still drawn to them, which makes it harder to focus.

It's more neuroscience: the fewer things we have distracting our brain in the periphery of our visual field, the more we can hunker down and direct our attention to what is most important in front of us. Make it easy for your eyes and for your brain, and cross those babies out.

However, you shouldn't be crossing off answer choices unless you are 95 percent sure they are incorrect. Otherwise, you could be shooting yourself in the foot.

Two Strategies for Every Section : *In Summary*

- If you are spending more than a minute on a question and still aren't close to solving it, circle it and come back to it after you get to the end of the section.

- Immediately cross out answer choices you are sure are wrong.

- Don't ever eliminate an answer choice if you are unsure about it.

CHAPTER 4
The English Test

"The greater part of the world's troubles are due to questions of grammar."

– Michel De Montaigne

So, you hated reading shakespeare in school, you have no idea what the difference between a direct and indirect object is, and the last essay you turned in to your English teacher was copied and pasted from Wikipedia. Well, I have good news for you: you can still dominate the English section.

Truth be told, 98 percent of the questions on the English test don't have anything to do with literary devices, plays by some Englishman, or knowledge of obscure grammatical rules. Instead, we can master the English section by studying and repeatedly applying the several rules and strategies we'll talk about in a minute.

Before we begin, you should know...

1. ### There Are Two Types of English Questions

   First off, it's important to know that all 75 questions on the English section can be classified in one of the two following categories

   1) Grammar Questions (The ACT calls this "Usage and Mechanics")
   2) Style Questions (The ACT calls this "Rhetorical Skills")

   Grammar questions will test your knowledge of verb tenses, punctuation, pronouns, and the ilk. Errors such as 'Me are hungry.' fall into this category Grammar questions will test things as simple as "their" vs. "there", or as tricky as "who" vs. "whom".

   Style Questions, unlike grammar questions, test your ability to recognize run-on sentences, redundancy, unnecessary words, etc. The idea is this: a sentence can be completely grammatically (mechanically) correct, but still have room for improvement. The ACT is testing to see if you can tell if the sentence is the best it can be or if improvements can be made.

2. ### Questions Are Not Ordered by Difficulty

   In the English section, there is no particular order to the difficulty of questions — it is totally random.

3. **You Need to Work Quickly and Diligently**

Many students overestimate the amount of time they have and take the questions too slowly. Work quickly and diligently from the beginning of the section to avoid falling into this trap.

4. **Not Every Strategy and Concept Has Practice Problems**

You are about to see a list of the most important strategies and concepts to know for the ACT English test. Some of these, like 'Subject-verb agreement', require a little more practice in order for you to master them. For these, I've written practice problems to help you learn them better. Others like "One vs. You" or "Might've, Could've, Would've…" will be easier to pick-up and don't require practice problems.

THE 14 WAYS YOU WILL CONQUER THE English TEST

1. Subject-Verb Agreement

We have to make sure the subject and verb of the sentence agree with one another.

If your subject is singular, your verb must be singular.
If your subject is plural, your verb must be plural.

This is why *"The dog are hyper."* sounds atrociously incorrect.

While this error is glaringly obvious, these errors are harder to catch on the English test. However, there are two ways we can make sure we always have subject-verb agreement.

Way #1: Cross Out Prepositional Phrases

> 44. The team of baseball players <u>is</u> happy.
>
> A. NO CHANGE
> B. are
> C. were
> D. have been

The above question is testing to see if you can tell if the verb is in the correct form. But before we can know the correct verb, we have to know the noun, or subject, it's referring to.

Most of the time, the ACT likes to trick you by putting a prepositional phrase in between the subject and the verb to confuse you. To see this, let's grammatically break down the sentence in the above example.

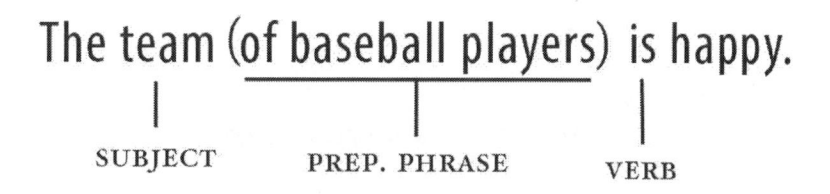

The team (of baseball players) is happy.
    SUBJECT   PREP. PHRASE   VERB

What *is* happy? Is it the baseball players?

No! It's the team. The prepositional phrase "of baseball players" just tells us what kind of team it is. What kind of team is it? It's a team of baseball players!

A useful trick here is to cross out the prepositional phrase in any sentence and make it exponentially easier for us to see which answer is correct.

The team ~~of baseball players~~ is happy.

"*The team is happy.*" makes sense. On the other hand, "*The team are happy.*"? Not so much.

If you're wondering what a prepositional phrase is, it's just a descriptive phrase that follows a preposition.

10 MOST COMMON PREPOSITIONS IN ENGLISH

of	on
in	at
to	from
for	by
with	about

While these are the ten most common prepositions in the English language, there are many more you can review by googling "*list of prepositions*".

For some more practice, here are some sample sentences using the above prepositions. The subject and the verb are **bolded**, while the prepositional phrase is *italicized*.

Sandwiches *from New York* **are** the best

The March *of Dimes* **is** a great cause.

Romeo and Juliet *by Mrs. Talbot's class* **was** the best school production overall.

In summary, by crossing out the prepositional phrase, we can make matching the subject and the verb a much easier task.

Way #2: Cross Out Info Bounded by Commas (or dashes)

Additional information bounded by commas should also be crossed out when determining the subject-verb agreement. For example, take the following sentence:

My mom, who grew up in Bogotá with her three sisters, like cream cheese.

To the average person reading this sentence, there might not seem to be any obvious errors. However, what the ACT has done here, is made the verb match up with the information right before it, which is *not* the subject.

The main idea of the sentence is not "three sisters like cream cheese." It's *my mom* who likes cream cheese.

Phrases bound by commas merely provide additional information about the subject. In the context of the passage, it might help to know that this individual's mom grew up in Bogota with her three sisters. However, we should cross out these descriptive phrases to make sure the subject and the verb are truly matching.

My mom, who grew up in Bogota with her three sisters, like cream cheese.

Is "*My mom like cream cheese.*" grammatically correct? Absolutely not. By doing this, it becomes obvious that the verb should be a singular "likes" to match with the singular subject "mom".

If you always ask yourself which subject the verb is describing, there's no reason why you should ever have trouble with this type of question!

> NOTE: *Dashes are used interchangeably with commas. So our grammatically incorrect example might also appear as: My mom—who grew up in Bogota with her three sisters—like cream cheese.*

Subject-Verb Agreement: *In Summary*

- Always make sure the verb matches up correctly with the subject it's describing.

- Crossing out prepositional phrases can help you match the subject and the verb better.

- Crossing out comma-bound phrases can also help you do this.

Practice **Subject-Verb Agreement** Questions

List the subject and the verb of each sentence and correct the verb if necessary.

1. In the Renaissance-period book, Emily, alongside the merchants, decide to take matters into her own hands.

2. Skipping school, warned the Australian public service announcements, is an act that can have grave and unforeseen consequences, like accidentally finding yourself stuck in an abandoned minefield while you're supposed to be in class.

3. The litter of kittens were so happy to finally have an owner that cared for them well.

Additional **Subject-Verb Agreement** Questions in the *RACT Guide*

Test 1, page 156, #33
Test 1, page 159, #47
Test 3, page 444, #42
Test 5, page 721, #9
Test 5, page 721, #12
Test 5, page 728, # 58
Test 5, page 724, # 31

2. Keep it Short, Sweet, and Simple

Let's face it. We all know somebody who tries to act smarter than they are. They tend to use big words and create complicated sentences, even though they could express the same ideas using much simpler and more effective sentence structures.

This type of person is known as a *hipster*. **For example...**

Hipster version: *"That movie brought me such ebullience and enjoyment."*

Simple version: *"I enjoyed the movie."*

The ACT doesn't like hipsters...

The ACT prefers simple answer choices to complicated ones. Whenever you are presented with a series of answer choices, always pick the one that captures the core idea in a simple and effective sentence.

Often times you'll also notice that the **shortest answer choice is the simplest**, and therefore the **correct** answer. For example, look at the following question.

> I saw I had a missed call right as I turned onto my <u>street that was 36 feet wide.</u>
> 42

    A. NO CHANGE

    B. street which had many decorated mailboxes.

    C. street which was filled with garbage.

    D. street.

See how the last answer stands out visually from the others? All the other answer choices are much longer. They also happen to be more complicated, unnecessary, and in the eyes of the ACT, incorrect.

Irrelevant Answer Choices are Always Wrong

Something else you might have noticed about other, incorrect answer choices in the question above, is that they are all irrelevant. When considering answer choices we have to ask ourselves:

> *"Does it add to the purpose of the paragraph to know how wide the street was?"*

> *"Is it necessary information to mention how decorated or not decorated the mailboxes were?"*

> *"Will the reader miss out on important information if we neglect to mention the amount of garbage in the street?"*

Although we didn't have the context of the rest of the passage to make inferences, chances are the passage has absolutely nothing to do with any of these things.

. . .

Now, by no means are we saying you shouldn't use new words in your life to broaden your vocabulary. However, we want to avoid constructing incorrect sentences for the sake of sounding smart, right?

Just keep it short, sweet, and simple. The ACT doesn't need to be impressed.

Keep it Short, Sweet, and Simple: *In Summary*

- Answer choices that sound wordy or fancy are often incorrect.

- Look for the simplest answer choice.

- This is often, but not always, the *visually* shortest answer choice (fewest amount of words and letters).

- Keep in mind that answer choices that contain unnecessary, irrelevant information are also incorrect.

Additional **Short, Sweet...** Questions in the *RACT Guide*

Test 1, page 159, # 50
Test 2, page 292, # 4
Test 4, page 581, # 32
Test 5, page 721, # 7
Test 5, page 725, # 39
Test 5, page 730, # 71

3. Don't Be Redundant

This is a type of Style question that can slip right past you if you aren't paying attention. Read the following sentences.

I went kayaking in the water.

Karen drank a milkshake, made with milk.

I took a math test, covering several mathematical concepts.

She was not American, meaning she was a foreigner.

What do all of these sentences have in common? They're all redundant!

You have to be in the water to kayak, you have to use milk to make a milkshake, a Math test is going to test mathematical concepts, and if someone isn't American, they must be a foreigner!

If an answer choice repeats information that was previously stated or understood before, it's redundant and should be crossed out.

Don't Be Redundant: *In Summary*

- Cross out any answer choices that are redundant or repeat information that was previously stated.

Additional **Don't Be Redundant** Questions in the *RACT Guide*

Test 1, page 154, # 20   Test 3, page 445, # 49
Test 1, page 159, # 50   Test 3, page 447, # 67
Test 1, page 162, # 66   Test 4, page 586, # 66
Test 1, page 153, # 9   Test 4, page 586, # 68
Test 2, page 297, # 34   Test 5, page 720, # 3
Test 3, page 444, # 41   Test 5, page 730, # 71

4. Odd One Out

If you are given several things that are similar and one that is different, it is usually fairly easy to recognize the outlier.

Sometimes on the ACT you're given a question that has three similar answers and one that's different. Since the three similar answers are practically the same, the answer choice that's different must be the correct one. For example...

35. *How do most students feel when school is cancelled because of snow?*

    A. depressed
    B. angry
    C. hopeless
    D. absolutely wonderful

The first three answer choices are all negative (as well as false) descriptions, whereas the last is the only positive description. If hypothetically, answer choice A were correct, why couldn't answer choice B or C be correct as well?

A more typical "Odd One Out" ACT will offer answer choices like these...

    A. but
    B. however
    C. yet
    D. therefore

Which one of these is the odd one out? That's right. It's answer D!

All the other answer choices are words that change the direction of the sentence. If "but" were correct, why couldn't "however" or "yet" also be correct? They all begin an idea that contrasts with the idea in the preceding sentence. Because the odd one out here, "therefore"' is the only one that continues the idea and doesn't contrast it, it is the only possible correct choice.

Notice how we didn't even have to look at a question to figure out which one of these answer choices was correct. That is exactly how powerful this strategy is.

Odd One Out: *In Summary*

- Some questions on the ACT English section have three answer choices that are very similar to one another and one that is different.

- If one of the three similar answers were correct, then the other choices could be correct as well.

- The odd one out is usually the correct answer choice in these situations.

Additional **Odd one Out** Question in the *RACT Guide*

Test 1, page 159, # 52   Test 4, page 584, # 54
Test 3, page 444, # 48   Test 5, page 726, # 43
Test 3, page 443, # 33   Test 5, page 729, # 63

5. The Semicolon Test

This is one of the most important grammar rules for the ACT and for writing in general! Unfortunately though, for eons, most English teachers across the country have neglected to clearly explain how this bad boy is used. So, let's try to break it down.

The semicolon has two common usages.

1) **To separate two independent clauses**

   Ex: *She studied for the ACT consistently each day for 6 weeks; therefore, when she scored a 32 on the test she wasn't surprised.*

2) **To separate items in a list** (locations, names, dates, and descriptions.)

   Ex: *This summer, I got the chance to travel to San Juan, Puerto Rico; Berlin, Germany; Zurich, Switzerland; and Auckland, New Zealand.*

It's important to note the following fact:

THE ACT ONLY USES SEMI-COLON USAGE #1

Keeping that in mind, how do we check to see if a semicolon is being used correctly anyway? Funny you should ask...

> **ACT Semicolon Usage:** *To separate two independent clauses*

While words "independent clause" might seem complicated, all the phrase means is a *string of words that can stand on its own.*

To check if a semicolon is used properly, make sure that both parts of the sentence (*whatever comes before the semicolon* AND *whatever comes after the semicolon*) can stand on their own as full sentences. If each can stand on its own, the semicolon is correctly used and you're good to go! However, if not, you've got a fragment on your hands. And remember, complete sentences always have a **subject** and a **verb**.

Correct Semicolon Usage: *what comes before and after the semicolon can both stand on their own as complete sentences.*

- ✓ *Gabe's in a ska band called Crawford's Combover; I hear he's quite popular with the ladies.*

- ✓ *I went to the aquarium last week to see the dolphin fight; it was legendary.*

- ✓ *We were in total and utter disbelief when Johnny streaked across the football field during the band's halftime show; I'm glad I got it on tape.*

Incorrect Semicolon Usage: *either what comes before OR what comes after cannot stand on its own as a complete sentence.*

- ✗ *Wiley Papyrus' new album; bulldozer, was a huge hit with rebellious teenagers across the country.*

- ✗ *Then, she threw the milkshake in his face; being so rude.*

- ✗ *Atlantis is the fabled underwater city that was lost for centuries; resting at the bottom of the sea.*

The Semicolon Test: *In Summary*

- The only real semicolon usage on the ACT is to separate two independent clauses, or two strings of words that can stand on their own as full sentences.

- If each part on either end of a semicolon **cannot** stand on its own as a full sentence, then the semicolon is being improperly used, and you should cross out this answer choice.

Practice **The Semicolon Test** Problems
Determine which of the following sentences have a correctly used semi-colon.

1. While he wasn't exactly a police officer; he did have some background in law enforcement.

2. Sharon loved frozen yogurt, almost too much; she often woke up covered in dried fro-yo stains not knowing where she was or how she had gotten there.

3. The notebook fell in-between the night stand and the fireplace; it was hard to see.

Additional **Semi-colon Test** Questions in the *RACT Guide*
Note: the following questions contain both correct and incorrect semi-colon usage.

Test 1, page 154, #18	Test 2, page 297, #31	Test 5, page 720, #4
Test 1, page 157, #39	Test 3, page 441, #22	Test 5, page 724, #28
Test 1, page 162, #69	Test 4, page 581, #36	Test 5, page 725, #34
Test 2, page 293, #10	Test 4, page 583, #48	Test 5, page 727, #53
Test 2, page 295, #20	Test 5, page 720, #1	Test 5, page 729, #59

6. Tense

Remember: in any sentence the tenses of each verb must match up. When your answer choices have different verb tenses, look elsewhere in the passage for the verb tenses the author uses. This will give you a good idea of what tense your verb needs to be in.

What's that? You're having trouble remembering your future perfect from your past simple? No problem. Here is a quick reminder of the tenses using a dance move that's recently taken the country by storm.

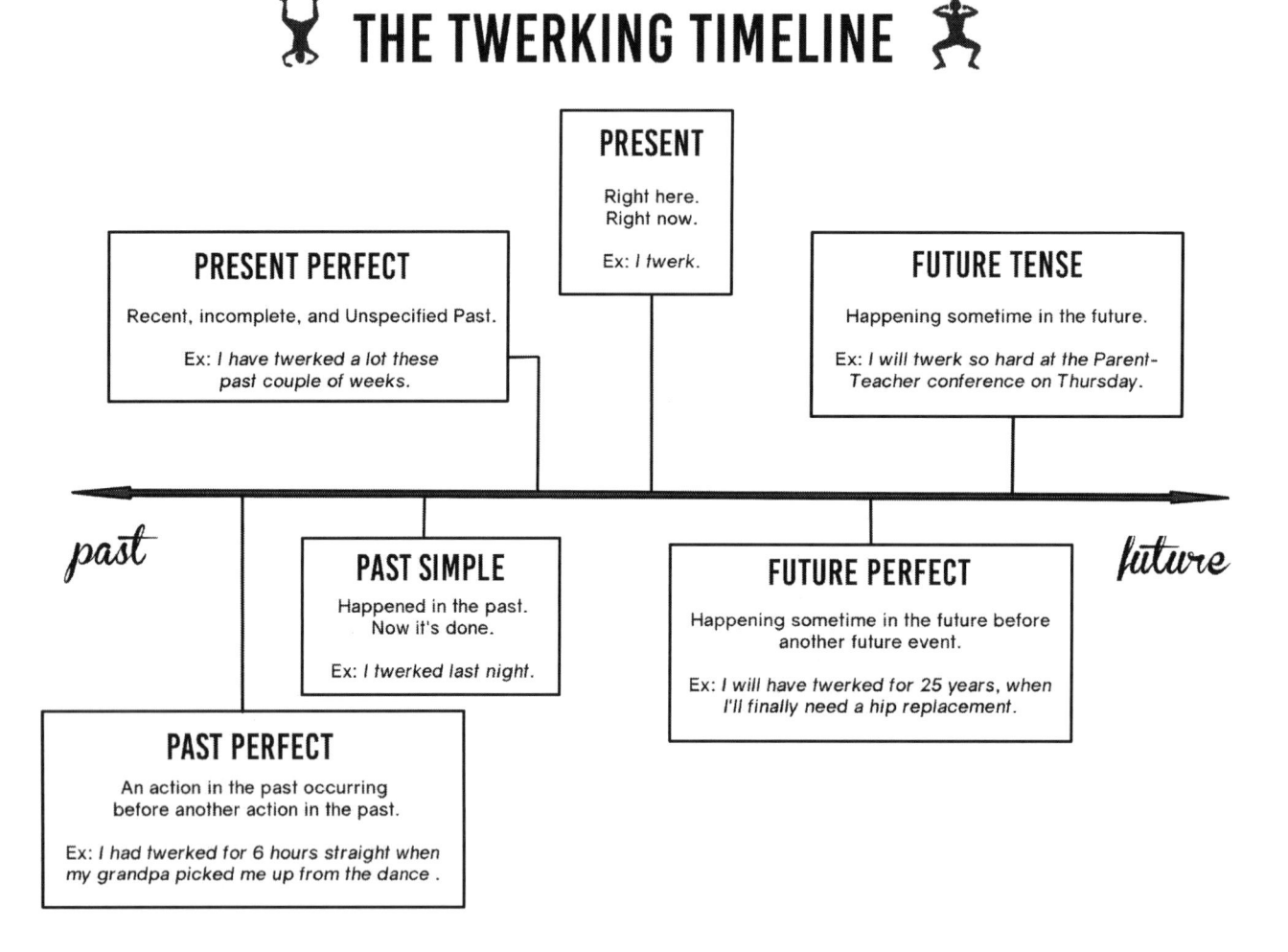

THE TWERKING TIMELINE

PRESENT
Right here. Right now.
Ex: *I twerk.*

PRESENT PERFECT
Recent, incomplete, and Unspecified Past.
Ex: *I have twerked a lot these past couple of weeks.*

FUTURE TENSE
Happening sometime in the future.
Ex: *I will twerk so hard at the Parent-Teacher conference on Thursday.*

past ← → *future*

PAST SIMPLE
Happened in the past. Now it's done.
Ex: *I twerked last night.*

FUTURE PERFECT
Happening sometime in the future before another future event.
Ex: *I will have twerked for 25 years, when I'll finally need a hip replacement.*

PAST PERFECT
An action in the past occurring before another action in the past.
Ex: *I had twerked for 6 hours straight when my grandpa picked me up from the dance.*

Two of the trickiest tenses to confuse are the past tense and the past perfect tense. Let's use the verb "to eat" to better describe the differences between these two:

> simple past: *I ate.*
> past perfect: *I had eaten.*

While they may seem similar, they are not interchangeable!

Simple past describes an action in the past.

> *A year ago, I **made** a sandwich, **left** it in the fridge, and **forgot** about it.*

> *Yesterday, I **remembered** about the sandwich, and **ate** it.*

> *An hour ago, I finally **left** the bathroom after the most painful 24 hours of my life.*

Past perfect, on the other hand, describes a past event in relation to **another past event**.

> *A year ago, I **had made** a sandwich I intended to eat when Guido **called** to ask me to bail him out of county jail.*

> *Yesterday, I **had planned** to make spaghetti for lunch, but my spaghetti maker **broke**, and I ate the sandwich instead.*

> *An hour ago, I **had spent** the whole day in the bathroom when finally I **started** to feel better.*

In each of these three sentences, the past perfect verbs ("had made" "had planned" and "had spent") give a point of reference for the other past simple events ("called" "broke" and "started") to occur.

Tense: *In Summary*

- When your answer choices have different verb tenses, look elsewhere in passage for the verb tenses the author uses; this will give you a good idea of what tense your verb needs to be in.

- Past simple (I ate, I talked, I spoke, I made, I drank) simply refers to an action in the past.

- Past perfect (I had eaten, I had talked, I had spoken, I had made, I had drunk) is the past of a past.

Practice Tense Problems

1. In the War of 1812, the British raze Washington D.C. in retaliation for the Americans razing Toronto.

2. I am excited for the concert tomorrow night because I loved Earth, Wind & Fire.

3. The little girl finished all the chocolate milk before her mother arrived home.

Additional Tense Questions in the *RACT Guide*

Test 1, page 155, # 22
Test 1, page 158, # 44
Test 4, page 577, # 7
Test 5, page 729, # 64

7. It's Irrelevant!

You always want to avoid answer choices that contain any irrelevant information.

By irrelevant I don't just mean irrelevant to the content in the passage. If I have a passage about recent advances in aviation, and I throw in a sentence dealing with chimpanzee anatomy, the sentence will obviously be irrelevant and an incorrect answer choice. This is too obvious.

No, the type of irrelevance that the ACT tests is much more subtle.

When considering answer choices you have to ask yourself the following questions:

> **1. What is the paragraph about?**
> *Be as specific as possible.*
>
> **2. Does this information fit in with the context of the paragraph?**
> *If the answer choice doesn't fit in, we must cross it out.*

Take the following paragraph about homemade parachutes for example.

"In 1912, a young Austrian man jumped off the Eiffel Tower with a crowd of reporters and onlookers watching from below. He was testing his own invention: a silk parachute suit pilots could use to safely fall to earth in case of a midair failure. It didn't work, and he fell nearly 200 feet to an instant death. <u>It is said human beings can fall 30 feet without significant injuries.</u>"

We now ask ourselves the following questions:

1. What is the paragraph about?

The paragraph is describing the scene of the man jumping off the Eiffel tower with his own parachute.

2. Does this information in question fit in with the context of the paragraph?

Although the underlined information is slightly relevant because it provides information about the distance humans can fall without injury, it still detracts from the main purpose of the paragraph: to describe the scene of the man jumping off the tower.

Verdict: *Cross it out!*

Relevance: *In Summary*

- What is the paragraph talking about? Does this information fit in with the context of the paragraph, or does it take away from the purpose of the rest of the paragraph? If it detracts meaning instead of adding meaning, cross it off.

Additional **Relevance** Questions in the *RACT Guide*

Test 1, page 152, # 5	Test 3, page 440, # 15
Test 1, page 153, # 8	Test 3, page 448, # 73
Test 1, page 158, # 43	Test 4, page 582, # 41
Test 1, page 158, # 46	Test 4, page 583, # 47
Test 2, page 292, # 5	Test 4, page 587, # 74
Test 2, page 295, # 18	Test 5, page 723, # 25
Test 2, page 301, # 56	Test 5, page 729, # 62

8. Maintain Parallel Structure

Read the following sentence and ask yourself if something seems off.

I love eating, sleeping, and watching soppy romantic films is nice too.

Did you catch it? Whenever we write out a list of things, whether those things are verbs, nouns, or adjectives, we have to make sure they are the same exact types of things, so they agree with one another. This is called parallel structure.

In the sentence above, we list three things: eating, sleeping, and watching soppy romantic films. The first two things are verbs ending in -ing. Up to that point, the sentence was just fine. However, the while the last verb starts with an -ing verb, it disrupts the flow by adding "is nice too" at the end. The fact that all three things listed are not the same parts of speech totally ruins the sentence.

By correcting the last item to agree with the others, we are left with:

I love eating, sleeping, and watching soppy romantic films.

Another way to think about parallel structure is to imagine that each type of thing is like a different social group in a cliquey high school. The goths, the nerds, the jocks, and the metal heads. All the metal heads are happy with the other metal heads, the goths are happy with the goths, so on and so forth. But, as soon as you go mixing and matching different cliques—one goth here, another jock there— you'll more than likely have a bloody mess on your hands.

I hope you can see how it the universe feels a little more at ease when we have full agreement among all the members of a list.

Parallel Structure: *In Summary...*

- If answer choice sentences have multiple items listed in a row, make sure that they agree with one another and maintain parallel structure.

Practice **Parallel Structure** Questions
Correct any sentences missing parallel structure.

1. He has taken his test, moved out of his parents' house, and also plans to travel to California in a few months

2. I'll believe his promises when he clarifies his vision, will deliver on his promises, and remains humble at the same time.

3. Sam didn't go out on Friday night but instead stayed home, heated up some mac and cheese, and decided to watch the "My Little Unicorn" DVD boxed set in its entirety.

Additional **Parallel Structure** Questions in the *RACT Guide*

Test 3, page 442, # 28
Test 5, page 721, # 12
Test 5, page 728, # 58

9. Who Loves Commas?

I certainly don't, and if I had to guess, I'd say neither do you.

Unfortunately for us, the ACT adores commas. So here are some rules for knowing which answer choice to pick when faced with a lot of different comma combinations.

Use a comma...

1. **...when listing three things.**

   When listing three things we want to place a comma after the first two items.

   I like bananas, mangos, and cherries.
   Her three children were named Alan, Maria, and Apple.
   I went to the store to buy prunes, adult diapers, and a beach shovel.

2. **...but NOT when listing two things.**

   When listing two things instead of three, no comma is necessary.

   Harold and Maude went to the grocery store.
   I brought an apple pie and ice cream for dessert.
   She was able to fight off the kidnappers using just a donkey and a cactus.

   ...unless the two things are two similar adjectives.

   Although you can't usually use commas to separate two things, you can of course they are two **similar** adjectives.

   He was a naive, inexperienced boy.

She was an annoying, overbearing neighbor.

3. ...*when sectioning off descriptive information.*

   As we saw in English Strategy number 1, sometimes additional descriptive information is placed in between commas in the middle of the sentence. This information is not crucial to the meaning of the sentence and in fact, could be pulled out without affecting the meat and potatoes of the sentence.

   My high school's lockers, in which I may or may not have been stuffed, are relatively cramped.

   Remember that dashes (—) can also section off descriptive phrases.

   My high school's lockers—in which I may or may not have been stuffed—are relatively cramped.

4. ...*when separating contrasting ideas or indicating a pause or shift.*

   The weather was unpredictable. It was sometimes hot, sometimes cold.
   He was merely naive, not stupid.
   She says she prefers to date short men, not tall men.

5. ...*with a short conjunction.*

   To extend a sentence to connect two independent clauses, you can use a comma along with a short conjunction (and, but, for, nor, yet, or, so)

   I love math, **but** *I'm not a fan of the way Mrs. Jenkins teaches it.*

   Marissa told me how she really felt, **and** *I appreciate her honesty.*

   I wasn't anxious about it, **yet** *I can't help but thinking about his horror story.*

*She just received her acceptance letter to Party U, **so** I guess she'll be going there.*

THE ULTIMATE COMMA RULE

To check if a phrase should be separated by a comma or not:

1. Read the phrase repeatedly in your head.
2. Audibly whisper the sentence.

While all of the other rules will be helpful for the ACT English section, as well as your writing in general, this rule is possibly the most effective of all. And isn't it beautiful how simple it is?

Your gut is a lot better at determining what should and shouldn't be separated by a comma than you think. After all, **commas only exist to separate ideas.** When you do this, pay attention to the most natural flow that your mind gravitates toward.

If you naturally pause in your head while reading something, there should probably be a comma. If you read through the sentence without pausing or hesitating even a bit, there should probably be no commas.

Is this strategy simple? Absolutely. But you would be surprised how often students pick an answer choice with incorrectly used commas just because they haven't done this.

Practice **Who Loves Commas?** Questions

Determine which sentences have inappropriately-used commas and make the necessary corrections.

1. The house, was around the corner, from the movie theater.

2. She, likes to drink coffee, unlike Jamie.

3. Jamie and his brother, decided to take the day off from work.

4. Last summer, I visited North Carolina, and New York.

Who Loves Commas?: *In Summary*

- Use commas when listing three things, placing a comma after the first two.

- Do not use commas when listing two things, unless they are similar adjectives.

- Commas or -em dashes (—) bounding a phrase are used to separate descriptive information.

- Use commas with a short conjunction (but, so, yet, etc…).

- Finally, use commas to separate contrasting ideas.

Additional **Who Loves Commas?** Questions in the *RACT Guide*

Test 1, page 153, # 7	Test 2, page 298, # 36	Test 4, page 579, # 20
Test 1, page 154, # 16	Test 2, page 300, # 52	Test 4, page 579, # 21
Test 1, page 154, # 18	Test 2, page 303, # 72	Test 4, page 580, # 27
Test 1, page 156, # 32	Test 2, page 303, # 75	Test 4, page 585, # 60
Test 1, page 157, # 39	Test 3, page 440, # 17	Test 4, page 586, # 69
Test 1, page 159, # 53	Test 3, page 441, # 21	Test 5, page 721, # 10
Test 1, page 161, # 61	Test 3, page 442, # 27	Test 5, page 727, # 50
Test 2, page 292, # 2	Test 3, page 445, # 54	
Test 2, page 293, # 7	Test 3, page 446, # 63	
Test 2, page 295, # 19	Test 4, page 576, # 1	
Test 2, page 296, # 26	Test 4, page 577, # 10	

10. To Introduce, Transition, and Conclude, Summarize!

How often do you finish reading something only to realize that you can't recall anything that you just read? When you think about it enough, you realize you weren't reading at all. You were just staring at pages with letters on them!

This happens to everyone at some point in time. Some of us (myself included) have a greater tendency toward doing this than others. It's important to make sure we're not doing this on the English section.

If you look at any relatively well-written story or text, you will notice that each paragraph serves a specific purpose and has a main idea. This is the case on the ACT, and we need to be aware of this.

It's important to understand the information in the passage but it's even more important to understand the purpose of each paragraph. To do so, I want you to ask yourself the following questions:

What purpose does the paragraph serve?

How does it relate to the paragraphs surrounding it?

There are **three** different types of questions on the English section for which this strategy is most useful.

Introduce - *Which answer choice would best introduce the paragraph?*

Transition - *Which answer choice would provide the best transition between paragraphs 2 and 3?*

Conclude - *Which answer choice provides a conclusion most consistent with the rest of the essay?*

So if we're reading a text about the life of George Washington, each paragraph might be summarized in the following way

Disclaimer: I do not claim to know anything about George Washington. All information below is purely speculation

Paragraph 1

George Washington had a great childhood.

Paragraph 2

His parents were really nice.

Paragraph 3

He eventually attended a military college.

Paragraph 4

Then he fought in the Revolutionary War. It wasn't all sunshine and rainbows, but he eventually led the American militia to victory.

Paragraph 5

After winning the war, he served as the first president of the United States and did lots of great things.

Paragraph 6

In summary, George Washington led a fruitful life filled with accomplishments and, because of this, is one of America's great historical figures.

There are tons of questions on the ACT that will gauge your understanding of paragraph topics. If you understand what you're reading, and can summarize it in one to two sentences, you will know which are the best introducing, transitioning, and concluding phrases.

Introducing, Transitioning, and Concluding: *In Summary*

- Some questions will ask you which sentence best introduces, transitions to, or concludes a paragraph

- For these questions, it's important to understand the information in the passage, but even more important to understand the purpose of each paragraph

- To do so, ask yourself the following questions:

    What purpose does the paragraph serve?

    How does it relate to the paragraphs surrounding it?

Additional **Introducing, Transitioning...** Questions in the *RACT Guide*

Test 1, page 154, # 15	Test 3, page 443, # 38
Test 1, page 155, # 24	Test 3, page 444, # 43
Test 1, page 157, # 38	Test 3, page 445, # 56
Test 1, page 160, # 54	Test 3, page 446, # 60
Test 1, page 161, # 64	Test 3, page 447, # 69
Test 2, page 294, # 13	Test 4, page 582, # 43
Test 2, page 301, # 53	Test 4, page 587, # 74
Test 3, page 439, # 4	Test 5, page 721, # 5
Test 3, page 441, # 20	Test 5, page 725, # 37
Test 3, page 441, # 25	

11. Avoid the Passive Voice at All Costs

Look at this picture of a robot holding a pencil. Don't ask questions…

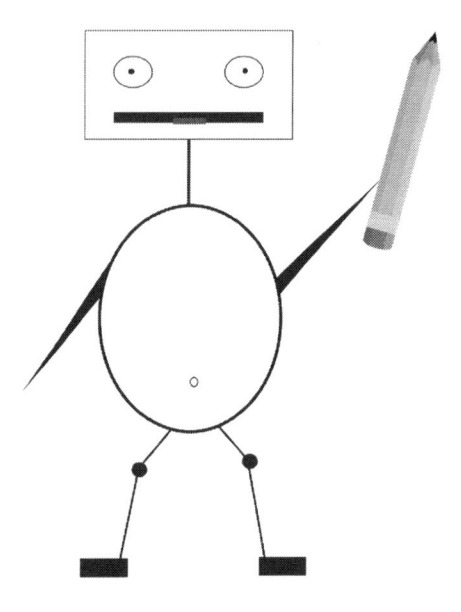

Look ma, I made a robot.

There are two ways we can focus on this picture:

The first is to focus on who is doing the action: the robot in the picture. So, if we zoomed in on him, we might write a sentence that reads: "**The robot** holds the pencil." This sentence places emphasis on the doer of the action and, because of this, is in the *Active Voice*.

*Active Voice: "**The robot** holds the pencil."*

The second way we could focus on this picture is to focus on the pencil, the object the action is done to. If we zoom in on the pencil that's being held and write a sentence about that, the sentence might read: "**The pencil** *is held by the robot.*" This sentence places the emphasis on the object, or the thing action is performed upon. This sentence is in the *Passive Voice*.

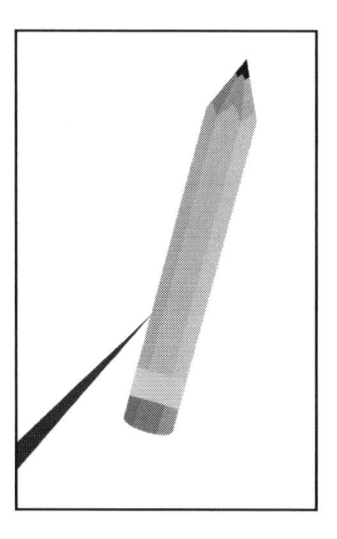

*Passive Voice: "**The pencil** is held by the robot."*

The ACT always prefers sentences in the active voice to those in the passive. So, whenever you see that an answer choice is in the passive voice, cross it out.

Luckily for us, there are some passive voice red flags we can watch out for to make it easier on us. All of the following are indicative of the passive voice and should be crossed out immediately.

AVOID THESE PASSIVE VOICE RED FLAGS

-being
-having been
-having -en, -ed (eaten, spoken, watched, talked, etc.)

Avoid the Passive Voice at All Costs: *In Summary*

- Sentences in the active voice are always preferable to those in the passive voice.

- "being" "having been" and "having -en, -ed" are indicative of the passive voice and should be avoided at all costs.

Practice **Avoid the Passive Voice at All Costs** Questions

1. What is the difference between the active voice and the passive voice? Which does the ACT prefer?

2. Determine which answer choices have the passive voice and correct them to active voice if necessary.

   a) He has never been to the Bahamas, this being the case because he was always too busy working.

   b) I took my Grandmother dancing with me last night; she might be old, but really knows how to move!

   c) Charlie, having been promoted to the rank of Sergeant, was elated.

3. What are the three passive voice red flags?

Additional **Avoid the Passive Voice...** Questions in the *RACT Guide*

Test 1, page 155, # 28
Test 1, page 156, # 34
Test 1, page 162, # 68
Test 2, page 294, # 12
Test 2, page 295, # 21
Test 2, page 295, # 23

Test 2, page 302, # 63
Test 2, page 441, # 22
Test 4, page 576, # 3
Test 4, page 581, # 38
Test 4, page 727, # 52

12. One vs You

The pronouns "one" and "you" are almost interchangeable. Almost.

One is used for more formal passages and texts. It gives off an air of formality and objectivity that distances the reader from the writer.

You is used for more casual and intimate writing. No, not that kind of intimate… Because of the personal nature of addressing someone with "you", using it can deliver a sense of **urgency** to the reader.

But, whichever pronoun we use, we have to make sure we're staying consistent in the passage and don't flip-flop around.

✓ **One** must brush his teeth if **one** would like to have a significant other.
✓ **You** must brush your teeth if **you** would like to have a significant other.
✗ **One** must brush his teeth if **you** would like to have a significant other.

Not a chance, my friend. Not a chance…

The first two sentences above are as good as gold. The last one is incorrect because it mismatches one and you.

In order to consistently get this right, always look at prior sentences and paragraphs in the passage to see how they're addressing the reader. If they use "you" in the beginning of the passage, they have to stick with it for the rest of the passage. The same goes for "one".

One vs. You: *In Summary*

- One is a more formal pronoun.

- You is a more personal pronoun.

- A passage can use either "you" or "one" when addressing the reader, but it cannot use both.

Additional One vs. You Questions in the *RACT Guide*

Test 1, page 160, # 56
Test 1, page 159, # 51

13. Its, it's, its'

One of these is a contraction for "it is," one of these is possessive, and one of these is an impostor, meaning it's not real.

Here are the proper usages.

its

MEANING: Possessive for pronoun "it"

EXAMPLE: *The dog adored its bone.*

it's

MEANING: Contraction for "it is"

EXAMPLE: *I hate the ACT. It's stupid.*

its'

MEANING: Nothing. This word doesn't exist.

EXAMPLE: *Never select its' as an answer on the ACT.*

As you can see, while the first two have real usages, the third does not exist and is grammatically incorrect. The ACT places it among the answer choices hoping you will get caught in the confusion and wrongly select it.

Almost every ACT test that I've seen has this question on it, but once you've seen it once, it's very easy to recognize

Its, it's, its': *In Summary*

- There is usually at least one question on the ACT English testing your knowledge of the three i-t-s.

- Its - possessive

- It's - contraction

- Its' - grammatically incorrect (don't pick this one!)

Practice **Its, it's, its'** Problems

Fill each blank with the correct version of i-t-s.

1. "____ so hard to find a boyfriend who will cook and clean for me!", Francine frantically exclaimed.

2. The parakeet isn't even mine, so why should I have to put up with ____ sass?

3. The orchid looks so happy in ____ new pot.

4. ____ crazy to think that even though it doesn't exist, ____ is chosen by many students on the ACT.

Additional **Its, it's, its'** Questions in the *RACT Guide*

Test 2, page 294, #17
Test 4, page 581, # 31
Test 5, page 723, #19

14. Might've, Could've, Would've...

Quickly, read the following sentences out loud and listen carefully:

Version 1: *If I had waited in line for a week, I might've gotten that big screen TV.*

Version 2: *If I had waited in line for a week, I might of gotten that big screen TV.*

Did you notice any difference in the pronunciation of these sentences? You shouldn't have. They sound exactly the same. Despite this, only one is correct. Which one, though?

The correct choice is version 1. While "might've" stands for "might have," "**might of**" is horrendously incorrect and would most likely give your English teacher an aneurysm if she ever saw you write it in an essay.

It's not too difficult to catch: The ACT is simply trying to to trip you up with the fact that the *"-ve"* contraction sounds identical to the word *"of"*. In any case, it's good to be aware of this question type so that you don't hesitate or second-guess yourself in the heat of the moment.

Keep in mind the ACT also tries to confuse "could've" and "would've" with "could of" and "would of"—the latter two being the incorrect variations.

Might've, Could've, Would've: *In Summary*

Word	What does it mean?
might've	might have
could've	could have
would've	would have
might of / could of / would of	A trap! These are grammatically incorrect

Additional **Might've, Could've...** Questions in the *RACT Guide*

Test 3, page 440, # 19
Test 5, page 729, # 64
Test 5, page 726, #42

TWO GENERAL ENGLISH SECTION STRATEGIES

1. Underline Keywords

Too often on the ACT English section we're given a question that looks like this:

" Which of the following true sentences, if inserted here, would best conclude the essay as well as maintain the positive tone established earlier in the essay?"

The two things here that are most important to us are **"best conclude"** and **"positive tone."** The other, excess words are not essential and can take our eyes off the prize.

After reading the question once, underline the important parts and cross out everything else. This can make a huge difference. Remember, you have limited time and we want to make it as easy as possible for focus and concentration.

In the above example I would underline: *"best conclude the essay"* AND *"maintain positive tone."* Everything else is unnecessary in order to understand what the question is asking.

2. Avoid Slang and Informal Language Like You Would Ebola

To get turnt. Keep it real. Just chillin'.

What do all of the above have in common? They're slang and should not be used on the ACT.

While slang and colloquialisms have their place in certain situations (like trying to impress your homeboys) steer clear of them on the test.

Because the test is made by people who, while wonderful in their own regard, wear turtlenecks in June and enjoy listening to Beethoven while drinking Shirley Temples, the ACT tends to be very formal and proper.

When in doubt about whether an answer choice is formal enough, ask yourself if you would include it in an essay that you might turn into this English teacher. If not, cross it out.

When in doubt about an answer choice, ask yourself: would this English teacher approve of it?

CHAPTER 5
The Math Test

"If you stop at general math, you're only going to make general math money."

—Snoop Dogg

Let's be real: math doesn't have the reputation of being the coolest school subject. If math were a kid in your high school, he probably wouldn't be picked first for dodgeball. Or second. Or third…

But who cares about popularity anyway? Math is important for engineering, architecture, physics, chemistry, finance, and well… the ACT! And if we're being totally honest, there's nothing more attractive than a member of the opposite sex who's able to recite the equation for a circle by heart.

Love it or hate it, you have to know your way around several mathematical concepts in order to get a decent score on this section. However you may feel about this notorious section, I hope to show you that it's really not so bad after all.

Before we begin, you should know…

1. Math Pacing

Although the Math section is 60 minutes for 60 problems, don't make the mistake of thinking that each question will take one minute.

The difficulty level of the questions increases as you get further into the section, which means question 1 is the easiest and question 60 is the hardest. Because of this, the first 30 problems are going to take significantly less time than the last 30.

Many students don't realize this during the test. They are lulled into a false sense of security by how easy the first couple of questions are, and when they get to question 40 and have ten minutes remaining they're left making this face.

Work quickly through the Math Section, or else…

If you plan on finishing every question in the math section, a good estimate to go by is finishing the first 30 questions in less than 20 minutes and leaving 40 minutes for the last 30.

However, for some students aiming for a score of 25, and not a 32, it might not make sense to try and answer the last 10 questions.

Think about it. To get a 25 on the Math section you need to answer roughly 40 questions correctly. What are the 40 questions you have the greatest chance of answering correctly? The first 40, of course. You don't want to rush through the Math section to try and answer every question if doing so will cause you to rush and decrease the likelihood you'll correctly answer the easier questions.

2. You Must Memorize the Formulas

Unlike the pre-2016 SAT, you are not given a formula sheet at the beginning of the math section for reference. All the math equations you use will have to be those that come from your head.

In the beginning of the next section is a formula sheet with all the equations you must memorize. No excuses! (*And don't feel too bad about it, because anyone who takes the SAT seriously has to memorize these too...*)

3. The Greatest and Most Underrated Math Strategy

Draw! Diagram! Mark up your problem! Write out your work! Believe it or not, this is the greatest strategy you can bring to the Math section.

This is a simple strategy, but I can't stress it enough. Out of the hundreds of students I've worked with, too many of them have this ridiculous belief that they are only truly intelligent if they can look at a problem and solve it in their head without writing anything out.

The fact of the matter is that the ACT Math section is a high pressure situation. You don't want your brain to have the unnecessary burden of holding information that could be written out on the page in front of you. By putting things down on paper, you free your brain to dedicate its energy to solving the problem.

Even as an expert of test prep, if I don't draw certain questions out, my chances of successfully solving the problem drop dramatically.

Don't be afraid to write in your test booklet. No one is collecting it, and you aren't any less intelligent for concretely visualizing the steps. But keep in mind, you should be writing out work because it helps you, not because you feel obligated to. This isn't math class and you won't lose any points for not showing your steps.

The best problem solving isn't an instant knowledge of knowing how to solve a problem, but rather a working process in which you take the information you've been given, and play around with it until the solution presents itself to you.

Remember: solving a problem in your head doesn't make you smarter, but getting a problem wrong because you didn't write it out will definitely make you feel stupid.

What you shouldn't be drawing out

- Operations that you can easily do in your head (2*4, 10-5, etc.)

- Work done for the sake of work. (This isn't math class, and you don't get any points for showing work!)

What you should be drawing/writing out

- Any problem with a geometric figure that isn't already drawn

- Any mathematical operation you feel unsure about (If you're struggling to do 4*8 for whatever reason, use your calculator!)

- Brainstorming the solution to a problem you're working on

4. Make Sure Your Fundamentals Are Strong

Need to brush up on your math fundamentals? Two great free websites you can use to hone your skills are ixl.com and algebrarules.com. But make sure you're only practicing the math concepts you need for the test. The ACT tests the following subject-areas:

Pre-Algebra
Elementary Algebra
Intermediate Algebra
Coordinate Geometry
Plane Geometry
Trigonometry

And of course, if you're looking for even more specific guidance, you can always contact me.

THE 18 WAYS YOU WILL Conquer THE MATH TEST

ACT MATH EQUATIONS SHEET
Memorize these. No excuses!

COORDINATE EQUATIONS

distance formula $\sqrt{(x_2-x_1)^2+(y_2-y_1)^2}$

midpoint formula $\left(\dfrac{x_1+x_2}{2}, \dfrac{y_1+y_2}{2}\right)$

slope $m = \dfrac{y_1-y_2}{x_1-x_2}$

TRIG FUNCTIONS

Sin(x) = O/H

Cos(x) = A/H

Tan(x) = O/A

INVERSES

Cosecant(x) = H/O

Secant(x) = H/A

Cotangent(x) = A/O

CIRCLE EQUATIONS

area of a circle $A = \pi r^2$

circumference of a circle $C = 2\pi r$

Volume of a cylinder $V = \pi r^2 h$

equation of a graphed circle with center (h,k) and radius r $(x-h)^2+(y-k)^2=r^2$

MISCELLANEOUS STUFF

$\log_a b = c \longrightarrow a^c = b$

$a^{\frac{b}{c}} = \sqrt[c]{a^b}$

$(a^2 - b^2) = (a-b)(a+b)$

$\dfrac{\text{sum of items}}{\text{\# of items}} = \text{average}$

TRIANGLES

area of a triangle $A = 1/2(bh)$

pythagorean theorem $a^2+b^2=c^2$

SPECIAL RIGHT TRIANGLES

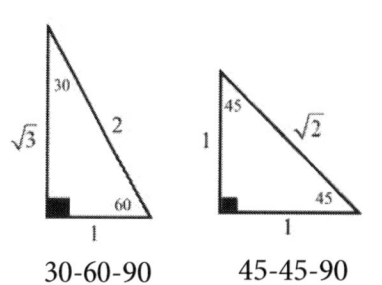

30-60-90 (sides: 1, $\sqrt{3}$, 2)

45-45-90 (sides: 1, 1, $\sqrt{2}$)

I Used to Hate the ACT, too. - Andre Kiss, *founder of* testpreplive.com

1. The Distance Formula

These are easy points on the ACT that you shouldn't be losing just because you forgot to memorize the formula.

To find the distance between two distinct points on a graph the equation is:

$$d = \sqrt{(x_2-x_1)^2 + (y_2-y_1)^2}$$

However, to understand it conceptually, we need to see that the distance equation is just a glorified version of the Pythagorean Theorem.

Understanding the Distance Formula

Follow me down this mathematical rabbit hole, to see the distance formula in a new light. When we square both sides we get

$$(x_2-x_1)^2 + (y_2-y_1)^2 = d^2$$

Does this look familiar?

$$(x_2-x_1)^2 + (y_2-y_1)^2 = d^2$$

$$a^2 \quad + \quad b^2 \quad = c^2$$

That's right. The distance formula is essentially the Pythagorean Theorem. Let me explain why with pictures using the points (6,5) and (1,1).

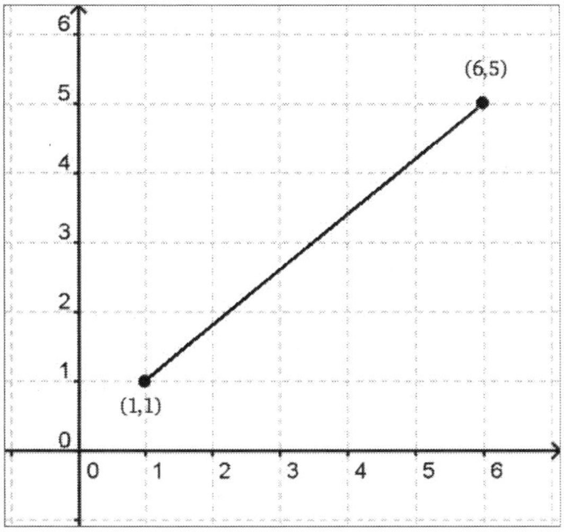
(6,5)
(1,1)

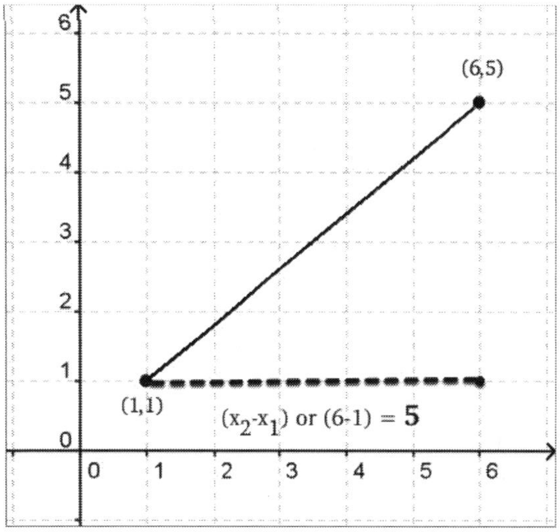
(6,5)
(1,1)
(x_2-x_1) or (6-1) = 5

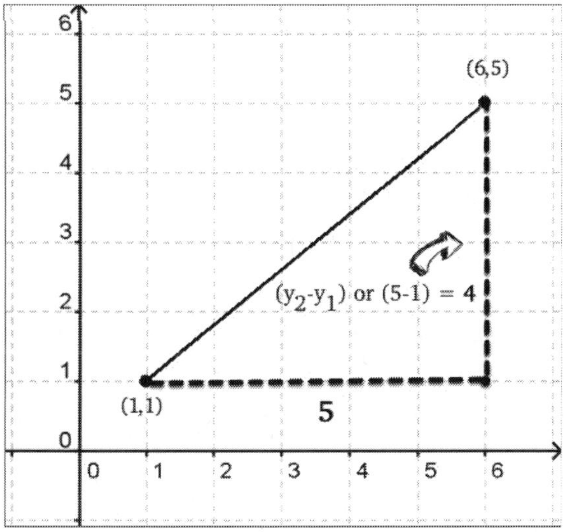
(6,5)
(y_2-y_1) or (5-1) = 4
(1,1)
5

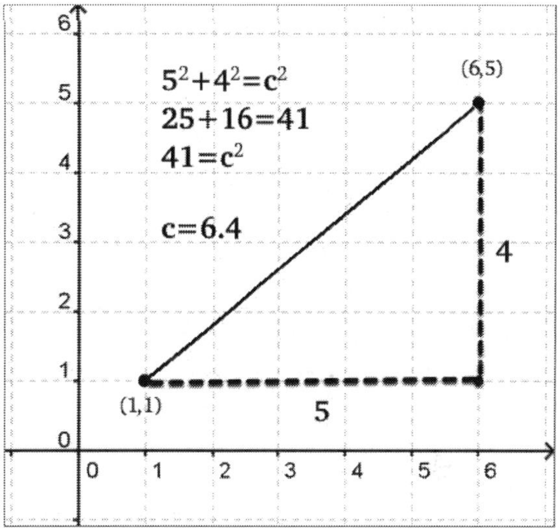
$5^2+4^2=c^2$
25+16=41
$41=c^2$
c=6.4
(6,5)
4
(1,1)
5

Am I showing you this so you can impress cute boys and girls at parties? That too. But the real reason is so that you can more easily remember the distance formula, and where all of those +, –, and $^{2\text{'s}}$ are.

Distance Formula: *In Summary*

- There is usually at least one question on the ACT that is a simple distance formula plug and chug, and these are easy points.

- Remembering that the distance formula is essentially a glorified pythagorean theorem can help you more easily memorize it.

Practice **Distance Formula** Questions

1. Find the distance between (-3,5) and (2,10)

2. Find the distance between (2,1) and (6,5)

3. Marge and John both leave Bob's house to go to their respective homes. Marge walks 3 miles north and 2 miles west. John walks 6 miles west. What is the distance in miles between Marge's and John's houses?

Additional **Distance Formula** Questions in *RACT Guide*

Test 1, page 174, # 45
Test 3, page 459, # 38
Test 5, page 739, # 31

2. Never Work in Fractions

Whenever you're given a mixed number, or a number in a fraction, change it to a decimal. Why? Because when we work with fractions we have to…

- find common denominators

- change mixed numbers to improper fractions

- add extra parentheses around the fraction in your calculator

All of these things not only take more time to do, but also introduce a greater margin of error (having more things to do means you're statistically more likely to make a mistake.) Either way, working in fractions is costing you points.

So, when you see a problem like this…

$$2\frac{5}{7} + x = 3\frac{3}{8}$$

…you should type in 5/7 and 3/8 in your calculator to see what those fractions are in decimal form. Then re-write the equation as so and solve for x.

$$2.714 + x = 3.375$$
$$x = 0.661$$

Change numbers with fractions to decimals as soon as you see them, and save yourself the headaches.

Never work in Fractions: *In Summary*

- Working in fractions is time-consuming and makes it easier to err.

- Instead of working in fractions in a problem, immediately convert them to decimals.

Practice **Never Work in Fractions** Problems

1. Jimmy, Johnny, Joe, and Alejandro work on a school project together. Jimmy contributes 1/5th of the work, Johnny contributes 3/8ths, and Joe contributes 2/7ths. What percentage did Alejandro contribute to the project?

2. Karen decided to bake a cake and the cake recipe calls for $1\frac{1}{2}$ cups of flour. However, she only has 3/4 of the flour required to bake the cake, so she decides to ask her neighbor for some flour. How many additional cups of flour will she need from her neighbor to bake an awesome cake?

3. John $5\frac{6}{8}$ feet tall and Jen is $5\frac{2}{5}$ feet tall. What is their approximate combined height in feet and inches?

Additional **Never Work in Fractions** Questions in the *RACT Guide*

Test 1, Page 164, # 1
Test 3, Page 453, # 16
Test 5, Page 732, # 1

3. Average (Also Known as the "Arithmetic Mean")

I'm sure everyone and their grandmothers know that to find the average of something you need to add up everything and divide by how many things you have. But because average problems aren't always so straightforward, I still want you to learn this equation.

$$\frac{\text{sum of items}}{\text{\# of items}} = \text{average}$$

We have to think about the above formula as an algebraic equation. Look at the following common problem as an example of what I mean…

> **54.** Ricky buys 5 coats at 5 different stores that cost 70, 68, 75, 46, and 80 dollars. What must the price of sixth coat at the last store in order for the average price of the coats to be 79 dollars?

We know how many coats we're looking for, and we know the average we're trying to get. The only thing we don't know is the cost of the sixth coat. This we represent with "x." When we plug in this information into the formula we get:

$$\frac{(70 + 68 + 75 + 46 + 80 + x)}{6} = 79$$

Once you have this set up, you can solve for x just like any other algebra problem.

$$70+68+75+46+80+x = 474$$

$$339+x = 474$$

$$x = 135$$

Average: *In Summary*

- Whenever you see you are working with an average problem, immediately write down this equation:

$$\frac{\text{sum of items}}{\text{\# of items}} = \text{average}$$

- Thinking of the average as an algebraic equation will help you solve these problems on the Math portion of the test.

Practice **Average** Problems

1. Class A has 60 students and Class B has 45 students. The same test is administered to both classes. Class A receives an average of 86 on the test, while Class B has an average score of 92. What is the average for both classes combined?

2. The Johnson boys (John, Ron, Brawn, and Don) are freakishly tall. John is 210 cm, Ron is 203 cm and Brawn is 195 cm. If the average height of all four boys is 200 cm, what is Don's height?

3. The average price of Nebraskan corn over 4 years is $23 per bushel (that's some expensive corn!). If the price of a bushel of corn was $27 the first year, what was the average for the next 3 years?

Additional **Average** Questions in the *RACT Guide*

Test 1, page 164, # 4
Test 1, page 167, # 14
Test 2, page 304, # 4
Test 3, page 450, # 1
Test 5, page 744, # 50

4. Combinations

While I'm not going to go in-depth about probability topics in this book (because most of the ACT probability questions are quite simple), the one thing I do want to discuss is combinations.

When you're mixing and matching distinct categories to see how many possibilities you can come up with, you're dealing with a combinations problem. They're quite simple.

To find the total number of possibilities, just multiply all the numbers from each category together.

So for example, if you're talking about different ice cream sundae combinations with *4 flavors, 5 toppings and 2 cones...*

(**4** flavors) × (**5** toppings) × (**2** cones) = **40** different sundaes

You would have 40 different possible sundaes.

If you're talking about different outfit combinations with *3 hats, 2 shirts, and 5 pairs of jeans...*

(**3** hats) × (**2** shirts) × (**5** jeans) = **30** different outfits

You would have 30 different possible outfits. Remember to multiply and you'll never get another combinations problem wrong again.

Combinations: *In Summary*

- Whenever a question asks you to find the total amount of possibilities of a multiple distinct categories, it's a combinations problem.

- To find the total number of combinations, simply multiply all the numbers from each category together.

Practice **Combinations** Problems

1. Easton High School is holding a raffle for concert tickets to go see U2 in concert. They will raffle off one ticket to a male student, one ticket to a female student, and one ticket to a teacher. If there are 150 male students, twice as many female students, and 20 teachers, how many different combinations of ticket-winners are there?

2. Brandon wants to look fly for work. He has 5 fly shirts, 2 fly pairs of pants, and 12 fly pairs of shoes. How many different fly outfits can Brandon wear to work today?

3. Artemis Faragorn is preparing for battle. He has 3 swords, 6 chainmail vests, and 2 shields, but may only use one of each on the battlefield. In how many different ways can Artemis charge into battle?

Additional **Combinations** Questions in the *RACT Guide*

Test 1, page 168, # 18
Test 2, page 309, # 24
Test 3, page 452, # 13

5. Get Concrete!

Any math problem is harder to solve when we are working with abstract terms than when we use real, concrete numbers. By using something concrete, you greatly increase the probability of selecting the right answer choice.

There are two ways we can get concrete with math problems.

1. Pick Some Numbers

When we aren't given specific numbers to work with, we can pick our own numbers to substitute in and solve for the answer. After seeing what that answer is, we can plug in our numbers into the answer choices and see which one matches up with what we got.

I know that sounds a little confusing, but let me offer you some clarity.

25. If x years ago Ivan was y years old, how old will Ivan be next year?

A. *x-y*
B. *(x+y)/y*
C. *(y-x)*y*
D. *x+y+1*
E. *5+x-y*

In the problem above we're given x and y. However, the fact that that we are given variables to work with instead of concrete numbers makes the problem unnecessarily difficult.

So, what can we do? Let's pick some numbers.

Let's say x=5 and y=30. In the context of the problem, this means that 5 years ago Ivan was 30 years old. That would make him 35 years old currently and 36 the next year.

So, the answer that we get when using x=5 and y=30 is **36**.

Now, we want to plug in our selected numbers of x=5 and y=30 into the answer choices and look for the answer that will gives us **36**.

Let's check the answer choices now.

A. 30-5 = 25   Incorrect
B. (5+30)/30 = 1.16666 Incorrect
C. (30-5)*30 = 150 Incorrect
D. 30+5+1 = 36 Gives us 36! Ding ding ding!
E. 5+5-30 = -20 Incorrect

Here we can see that answer choice D is the only one that gives us the number we were looking for.

You Can't Just Pick Any Numbers, Though

Instead of the original numbers we used, had we picked x=-30 and y=5, the problem wouldn't make any sense. That would mean that 5 years ago Ivan was -30 years old.

Additionally, the problem could state certain restrictions regarding the variables.

- *If it tells you that x and y are positive integers, don't pick negative or irrational numbers*

- *If it tells you that x is even and y is positive, make sure you are abiding by those restrictions*

- *Always make sure that the numbers you pick make sense in the context of the problem*

Make Sure You Check Every Answer

Sometimes multiple answers can give you the answer you're looking for. This means that when you're plugging your numbers back in, don't immediately go with the first answer choice that matches up with the answer you got.

2. Use Your Answers

Everyone loves to complain about standardized testing, but it's really not so bad. And this is why: when you think about it, the answers to every question on the test are always right in front of you!

So on the Math test, when we are given **simple integers** as answer choices, we can actually plug them back into the question to see if they are correct.

x+y is a positive, even number, while x/y is an integer. What are the values of x and y?

A. x = 2, y =1
B. x = 2, y =-3
C. x =-5, y = 5
D. x = 5, y =-1
E. x =10, y = 6

This problem gives us two conditions to satisfy. The first is that x+y must be positive and even. The second is that x/y must be an integer. So let's use our answers to help us solve the problem.

A. x+y= 3   (x+y is positive but not even. Cross it out!)
B. x+y= -1   (x+y is not positive. Cross it out!)
C. x+y= 0   (x+y is zero, neither positive nor negative. Cross it out!)
D. x+y = 4   (x+y is positive and even)   x/y= -5 (It's an integer!)
E. x+y = 16   (x+y is positive and even) x/y = 1.666 (Not an integer. cross it out!)

Get Concrete: *Summary*

- Picking numbers and using your answer choices can be extremely helpful when you're not given concrete numbers to work with.

- You want to pick easy numbers to work with, whenever you…

    1) …aren't given numbers to work with.

    2) …have variables in your problem you can test with real numbers.

- When we have simple numbers in our answer choices, we can actually use the answers to solve the problem

Practice Get Concrete Problems

1. A triangle has side lengths exactly twice the length of the smaller triangle. If the product of the sides of the smaller triangle is k, and the product of the sides of the larger triangle is h, what is h in terms of k?

    A. 2k
    B. 3k
    C. k²
    D. k+3
    E. 8k

2. Jeremy has twice as many nickels as dimes and 4 fewer quarters than dimes. If he has 36 coins, how many dimes does Jeremy have?

    A. 5
    B. 8
    C. 10
    D. 16
    E. 20

3. Martha buys a sweater for *d* dollars. Because Martha is the most popular girl in school, her wearing the sweater causes its value to appreciate by *h* percent. What is the value of the sweater, in terms of *d* and *h* after Martha wore it?

A. $d * 100/(h)$
B. $d + (h/100) * d$
C. $d(h+1)$
D. $d^2 + h^2$
E. $(100-h)/2d$

Additional **Get Concrete** Questions in the *RACT Guide*

Pick Some Numbers

Test 2, page 315, # 49
Test 3, page 456, # 27
Test 3, page 455, # 23
Test 3, page 465, # 57
Test 4, page 597, # 40
Test 4, page 599, # 48
Test 4, page 603, # 59
Test 5, page 737, # 26
Test 5, page 744, # 47

Use Your Answers

Test 2, page 306, # 14
Test 3, page 456, # 26
Test 5, page 736, # 18
Test 5, page 736, # 19
Test 5, page 737, # 22

6. Percent

What is a percent anyway? Percent literally means "for every hundred" (*per* means for, while *cent* means hundred). It's just a way to express quantities.

Simple Percent Problems

The formula for finding **x** percent of any number is actually quite simple. Memorize it.

$$\text{Original} \cdot (x/100) = \text{Final number}$$

In every percentage problem, you are always going to have one unknown variable. Sometimes your **final number** is unknown

Ex: *What is 23% of 72?*

$$72 \cdot (23/100) = \text{Final}$$

Other times, the **original number** is unknown

Ex: *48% of some number is 201. What is the number?*

$$\text{Original} \cdot (48/100) = 201$$

And other times, it's the **percent** is unknown

Ex: *What percent of 45 is 76?*

$$45 \cdot (x/100) = 76$$

It could be your original number, your percentage, or your final number. But regardless, you're always solving for some unknown variable.

Percent Increase or Decrease

If we want to find the percent change of a number, we use the following formula.

$$\text{Original} +/- [(\text{Original}) \cdot (x/100)] = \text{New}$$

For example...

A sweater priced at $50 is put on sale at a 32% discount. What is the new price of the sweater?

$$50 - [(50) \cdot (32/100)] = \text{Final Price}$$
$$50 - 16 = 34$$

The sweater initially costs 50 dollars.
32 percent of 50 is 16 dollars.
After the discount, the sweater costs 34 dollars.

Another example...

A store buys a microwave. The microwave doesn't sell at the original price at which the store lists it, so the price of the microwave is discounted at 20 percent. The microwave still doesn't sell, so when Black Friday comes along the microwave is put on sale at an additional 10 percent. By what percent is the microwave discounted from the original price?

As we just saw in "Get Concrete," whenever we're given a problem without specific numbers, we need to pick our own. Also, keep in mind that the easiest number to pick for percentage problems is 100. So, let's set the price of the microwave at $100.

1st discount: $100 - [(100) \cdot (20/100)]$ = Price after 1st discount
$100 - 20 = \$80$

2nd discount: $80 - [(80) \cdot (10/100)]$ = Final Price
$80 - 8 = \$72$

Pay attention to the fact that we needed to do this equation twice, the second time using the new price after the first year. Adding 20% and 10% does not yield the same result!

Percents: *In Summary*

- For simple percents problems: Original $\cdot$ $(x/100)$ = Final

- To find the percent change: Original +/- [(Original) $\cdot$ $(x/100)$] = Final

- When you aren't given a number for something in a problem, like the price of a microwave, come up with numbers that are easy to work with with percentages, like 100 or 10.

Practice **Percent** Problems

1. 205 is what percent of 72?

2. Tuition at Party U is increased by 4% consistently every year. If last year's total cost of attendance was $54,000 dollars what will the cost of attendance be in 2 years?

3. Johnny, wanting to impress the ladies, decides to buy a new convertible. However, Johnny neglects to take into account the car's depreciation (loss of value). As soon as he drives the car off the lot, it depreciates 15%. After the first two years, it then depreciates another 30%. By what percent did the value of the car decrease from before Johnny bought it to the end of the second year?

Additional **Percents** Questions in the *RACT Guide*

Test 1, page 174, # 44
Test 2, page 319, # 60
Test 3, page 465, # 60
Test 4, page 600, # 50
Test 4, page 600, # 52

7. Plug n' Chug

Confusion: From the moment your older siblings tried to convince you that you were adopted to the day you went to Chinatown for the first time, it's something we've all felt. And it's something the ACT tries to use on some math problems that we will call **Plug n' Chug**.

In these problems, they present us with an equation that seems as complicated as…

$$H = -B_e(1+\delta A_B)\frac{d^2}{d\xi'^2} + \frac{B_e(1+\delta A_B)}{(1+\xi')^2}\left(1+\sum_{i=1}^{\infty}\delta r_{iq}\xi'^i\right)J(J+1)$$
$$+ \frac{[\omega_e(1+\delta A_\omega)]^2}{4B_e(1+\delta A_B)}\xi'^2\left(1+\sum_{i=1}^{\infty}a_i(1+\delta A_{aiq})\xi'^i\right)$$

When in reality, it's more like this…

$$F = C * (9/5) + 32$$

The ACT presents you with these complicated-looking equations, hoping that you'll freak out. The reality is that these are much simpler than they make it out to be.

Whenever you see this type of problem, if you take a couple of deep breaths and remember the following steps, you'll be just fine.

1. *You don't need to have any prior knowledge about this formula. It's simply plug and chug.*

2. *To solve the plug and chug, we have to first define the variables. What does the problem tell us each variable stands for?*

3. *Once we define the variables, insert (plug) the given variables into the equation, and then solve (chug) for the unknown. There's always just ONE unknown!*

Practice **Plug n' Chug** Problems

1. Force is defined by the equation F = (m*vf - m*vi) /t where F=force, m = mass, vf = final velocity, vi = initial velocity, and t = time. If Johnny's remote controlled car is traveling 60 m/s and has a mass of 2 kg, what is the amount of force that would be required to stop his car in 5 seconds?

2. Elastic potential energy is defined as PE = 1/2kx^2, where PE is potential energy, k is the spring constant, and x is the length of extension or compression in meters. If the potential energy of a spring stretched .5 meters is 500 joules, what is its spring constant?

3. The time in seconds of each swing of a pendulum is defined by the following equation, where L is the length of the pendulum in meters and g is the acceleration of gravity. If L = .5 meters and g=9.8 m/s^2, what is T?

$$T = 2\pi\sqrt{\frac{L}{g}}$$

Additional **Plug n' Chug** Questions in the *RACT Guide*

Test 1, page 166, # 11
Test 1, page 170, # 26
Test 2, page 305, # 8
Test 2, page 308, # 22
Test 2, page 311, # 32
Test 3, page 458, # 34

8. Slope

Slope is simply a measure of the rate of change of a line. We use the following formula to find the slope of a line.

$$y_2-y_1/x_2-x_1$$

(also known as Rise/Run or $\Delta y/\Delta x$)

Slope is the "m" term in the slope-intercept form.

$$y = \overset{\text{slope}}{m}x + b$$

Parallel Lines Have the Same Slope

- $y=3x+4$ and $y=3x-10$ both have a slope of 3 and therefore are parallel lines

Perpendicular Lines Have Slopes that are Negative Reciprocals

- $y=3x+4$ and $y=-1/3x+10$ have a slope of 3 and $-1/3$ respectively and therefore are perpendicular lines

---

Important Note: *Whenever you see the words 'parallel' or 'perpendicular' in a problem, write down the slope formula. Chances are you'll need it!*

Some Basic Facts About Slope

A. Larger slope values represent steeper slopes.

B. Smaller slope values represent more gradual slopes.

C. Horizontal lines like y=5 have a slope of 0.

D. Vertical lines have undefined slopes.

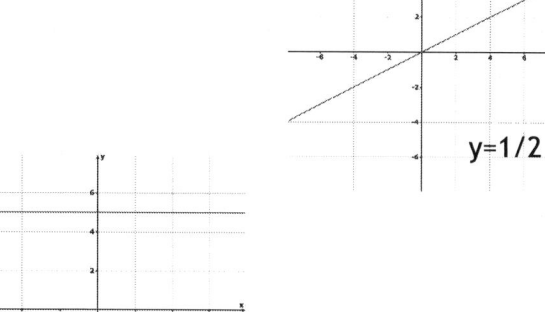

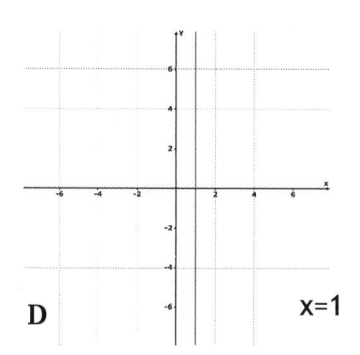

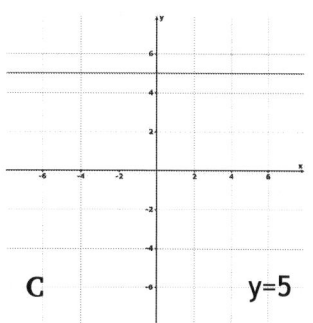

A y=5x

B y=1/2

D x=1

C y=5

Slope: *In Summary*

- Parallel lines have the same slope.
- Perpendicular lines have negative reciprocal slopes.
- If a problem mentions that lines are perpendicular or parallel, write down the slope formula; chances are you might need it.

Practice **Slope** Problems

1. What's the slope formula? (No cheating!)

2. Find the slopes of lines with the following points

   a) (0,0) and (7,-5)

   b) (2,4) and (13, 20)

   c) (10,-2) and (-5,-6)

3) Find the perpendicular slopes of a, b, and c.

9. Become a Master of y=mx+b

When we're dealing with the equation of a line, parabola, or other function on the ACT slope-intercept form is really the only form that matters.

As we saw earlier, slope-intercept form is...

$$y=mx+b$$

"y" is the y-coordinate, "m" is the slope, "x" is the x coordinate, and "b" is the y-intercept.

$$y=mx+b$$

- slope: m
- y-intercept: b
- y-coordinate: y
- x-coordinate: x

Whenever we see an equation that's not slope-intercept form, the first thing we need to do is isolate for "y" so that it is. Otherwise, the equation is useless to us.

3x-2y=16 *NOT in slope-intercept form*

y=3/2x-8 *INDEED in slope-intercept form*

y=mx+b: *In Summary*

- The only line form the ACT uses is slope-intercept form, so when dealing with equations in any other form, immediately change it to this.
- Slope intercept form is:

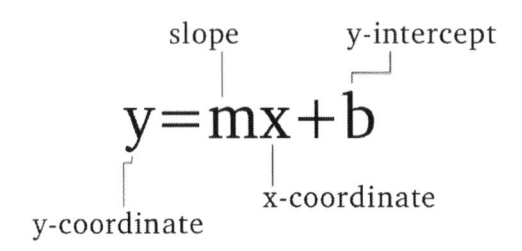

$$y = mx + b$$

where m is the slope, b is the y-intercept, y is the y-coordinate, and x is the x-coordinate.

Practice **Become a Master of y=mx+b** problems

For each of the following problems:

a) convert to slope-intercept form
b) find the slope of the line and of a line perpendicular to it
c) find the y-intercept

1. $5x+y-10=6$

2. $2y-3=4x$

3. $1/2x=16+4y$

Additional **y=mx+b** Questions in the *RACT Guide*

Test 1, page 169, # 22
Test 2, page 307, # 16
Test 2, page 308, # 19
Test 2, page 308, # 21
Test 3, page 453, # 17

Test 3, page 456, # 26
Test 3, page 462, # 48
Test 3, page 456, # 28
Test 4, page 593, # 26

10. Exponents

Let's start with the basic exponent rules.

1) When multiplying numbers with the same base, we add the exponents.

$10^6 * 10^5 = 10^{11}$

$x^4 + x^{20} = x^{24}$

$7^{4.5} + 7^{2.5} = 7^7$

2) When dividing numbers with the same base, we subtract the exponents.

$10^6 / 10^5 = 10^1$

$x^4 / x^{20} = x^{-16}$

3) When you see an exponent outside of an exponent, distribute.

$(x^2)^4 = x^8$

$(x^a)^b = x^{ab}$

4) Anything raised to the zero power equals 1.

$2^0 = 1$

$12805^0 = 1$

$a^0 = 1$

5) Anything raised to a negative exponent just means you put it under 1.

$2^{-5} = 1/2^5$

$4x^{-10} = 4 * x^{-10} = 4/x^{10}$

$x^{-2} = 1/x^2$

6) Memorize the form $a^{\frac{b}{c}} = \sqrt[c]{a^b}$

$2^{\frac{5}{3}} = \sqrt[3]{2^5}$

After you have mastered those, it's time to move on to the legendary exponent tip. Rumor has it that this very exponent tip was passed down from Jesus to his twelve disciples during the Last Supper. Are you ready for this? Are you sure?

Don't say I didn't warn you.

THE ULTIMATE EXPONENT RULE:

On the ACT, most terms with exponents can be put in base 2 or 3.

If you see an exponent of 9,27,81, or 243 in the problem think base '3'.

For example: $9^3 * 27^2$ can be simplified to $(3^2)^3 * (3^3)^2$

If you see an exponent of 4,8,16,32,64, etc. in the problem think base '2'.

For example: $4^2 * 64^2$ can be simplified to $(2^2)^2 * (2^6)^2$

Using this knowledge, let's solve the problem $(2^x)(4) = 8^3$

$$(2^x)(4) = 8^3$$
$$(2^x)(2^2) = (2^3)^3$$
$$(2^x)(2^2) = (2^9)$$
$$x+2 = 9$$
$$x = 7$$

Exponents: *In Summary*

- Memorize the basic exponent rules to be prepared for any ACT exponent problem.

- Most terms with exponents on the ACT can be put in base 2 or 3.

Practice **Exponent** Problems

Solve for a

1. $2(a^4)^2 = 512$

2. $(4a-6)^0 = a$

3. $9^{3a} * 3^{2a} = 81$

4. The cube root of $8 = 8^{1/a}$

5. $13^7/13^a = 13^2$

6. $2^4 * 2^a = 32$

Additional **Exponents** Questions in the *RACT Guide*

Test 1, page 164, # 2
Test 3, page 453, # 18
Test 3, page 457, # 31
Test 5, page 732, # 2
Test 5, page 746, # 56

11. Logs: Exponents That Got Fancy

If you came here looking for a section about thick, cut-up pieces of tree trunks, I apologize for the disappointment.

These are the logs we will be talking about in this section.

$$\log_4 16x = 2$$

Though it may look fancy, in reality, a log problem is really just an exponent expressed in another form. Which means that

$$\boxed{\log_a b = c \longrightarrow a^c = b}$$

Using this rearranged form, we can easily solve the problem above.

$$\log_4 16x = 2 \longrightarrow 4^2 = 16x$$
$$16 = 16x$$
$$x = 1$$

Here are some other examples:

$$\log_{10} x = 3 \longrightarrow 10^3 = x$$
$$1000 = x$$

$$\log_x 8 = 3 \longrightarrow x^3 = 8$$
$$x = \sqrt[3]{8}$$
$$x = 2$$

This rearrangement is something you have to practice over and over until you remember what goes where. Once you have it down, though, it will be second nature for you.

> **Important Note:** In our first example 'log₄16x=2' our base (or number in subscript) was 4. When you aren't given a number or a variable for your base, like 'log16x=2', it is implied that the base is 10.

Other, Uncommon, Log properties.

Because these aren't so common, and usually appear after question 45, these concepts might not be important unless you're trying to score over a 30 on the Math section.

1. *Numbers in front of "log" can be moved to be exponents for the number being log-ed.*

$$2\log(x) = \text{Log } x^2$$

2. *Just like with exponents, multiplication goes to addition.*

$$\text{Log } 2x = \log(2) + \log(x)$$

3. *And division goes to subtraction.*

$$\text{Log } 2/x = \log(2) - \log(x)$$

Log: *In Summary*

- A log is just an exponent in a different form

- The log rearrangement $\log_a b = c \longrightarrow a^c = b$ is simple, yet important

- For those looking to score above 30, memorize the uncommon log properties.

Practice Log Problems

Simplify

1. $2\log(x) + 2\log(y)$

Solve for x

2. $\log_5(3x-7) = 3$

3. $\log_2 8x - \log_2 4x = x$

Additional Log Questions in the *RACT Guide*

Test 2, page 319, # 59
Test 3, page 456, # 29
Test 4, page 599, # 49
Test 5, page 746, # 56

12. Functions

Functions in a Nutshell

Functions can seem confusing, especially when most of the math teachers who've tried to explain them to you are probably a little confused themselves.

The best way to think of any function is as a magical machine. The way that this magical machine works is when you put something in it, the machine changes it and spits out something different.

Original thing ——— *magical machine* —> *New thing*

An example of this would be a machine that takes a puppy and transforms it into a taco. Here are a couple of ways to think of a function.

Puppy ——— *magical machine* ——> *Taco*

Input ——— *function* ——> *Output*

x ——————*f*——————> *y or f(x)*

No puppies were harmed in the making of this book.

And just as there are tons of different magical machines— some that turn puppies into tacos, some that turn flowers into lampshades, and some that turn pencils into ice cubes—there are tons of different functions as well. Some functions take x and add 1, others multiply x by 5 and then subtract 3, others divide x by 100 and multiply by 6.

$$f(x) = x+1$$
$$f(x) = 5x-3$$
$$f(x) = (x/100)*6$$

Evaluating each function above with an x of 4 gives us the following.

$$f(4) = 4+1 = 5$$
$$f(4) = 5(4) - 3 = 20 - 3 = 17$$
$$f(4) = (4/100)*6 = 0.04*6 = 0.24$$

Evaluating Functions

Now we've got the basics down. But what do we do when we see something like…

Evaluate $g(x) = x^2 + 15$ when $g(4)$.

All this means is that everywhere we see x in the original equation, we plug in 4.

$$g(4) = 4^2 + 15$$
$$g(4) = 16 + 15$$
$$g(4) = 31$$

What if we evaluate $g(x+h)$?

It's the same idea here. This time, however, instead of plugging in 4 wherever we see x in the original function, we plug in (x+h). This looks like…

$$g(x+h) = (x+h)^2 + 15$$

$$g(x+h) = x^2 + 2hx + h^2$$

Function Transformations

When explaining function transformations, most tend to go into too much detail. I will keep it simple for you.

Shifting functions vertically is *intuitive* (+ shifts it up, - shifts it down), and it happens *outside* of parentheses.

Original Function: $f(x) = 20x$

Graph is shifted up three units: $f(x) = 20x+3$
Graph is shifted down three units: $f(x) = 20x - 3$

Shifting functions horizontally is *counterintuitive* (+ shifts it left, - shifts it right.) and it happens *inside* the parentheses

Original Function: $f(x) = 20x$

Graph is shifted right three units: $f(x) = 20(x-3)$
Graph is shifted left three units: $f(x) = 20(x+3)$

I use the word intuitive because one would naturally expect that adding a number would shift the graph in a positive way. Vertical shifts are intuitive. Horizontal shifts are not. Don't worry about why this is. For our intents and purposes, it's not important to know the reason why. Just study and remember the above information.

It's helpful to memorize this information, but if you're ever in a pickle and can't remember your function transformations, just enter the equations into your graphing calculator and compare them. Is the graph of the first equation higher or lower than that of the second? Is it wider or narrower?

Functions: *In Summary*

- Functions really aren't so scary. They are just magical machines that take in an input and spit out an output.

$$\text{Input} \quad \text{------ function ------>} \quad \text{Output}$$
$$x \quad \text{-------} f \text{--------->} \quad y \text{ or } f(x)$$

- To evaluate a function using a new input, simply plug in the input everywhere you see x in the original function.

    ex: If $f(x) = x^2+2x+17$ what is f(unicorn)?

    $f(unicorn) = (unicorn)^2 + 2(unicorn) + 17$

- Transforming functions vertically happens outside of the parentheses and is **intuitive** (+ shifts it up, - shifts it down).

    $f(x) = 20x + 5$: Graph is shifted up five units.

- Transforming functions horizontally happens within the parentheses and is **counterintuitive** (+ shifts it left, - shifts it right).

    $f(x) = 20(x-5)$: Graph is shifted right five units.

- If you're ever unsure about a function transformation, just graph both the original and the new function in your graphing calculator to easily see the transformation.

Practice **Functions** Problems

1. If $f(x)=10x+35$, what is $f(-4)$?

2. If $g(x) = (x+5)/7$ What is $g(f(2))$ if $f(x)=x+21$?

3. $f(x) =x^2+10$. How would the graph of $f(x)+3$ be different from $f(x-3)$?

Additional **Functions** Questions in the *RACT Guide*

Test 1, page 177, # 56
Test 2, page 309, # 23
Test 4, page 590, # 11
Test 5, page 732, # 3
Test 5, page 747, # 60

13. Angles and Angle-Algebra

Opposite Angles

Angles opposite each other have the same measure. Good stuff to know.

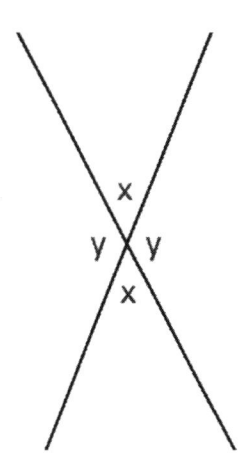

Transversals

As some of you may recall, if we have two lines that are parallel to one another, and another line intersects these two, there are some things we can assume to be true.

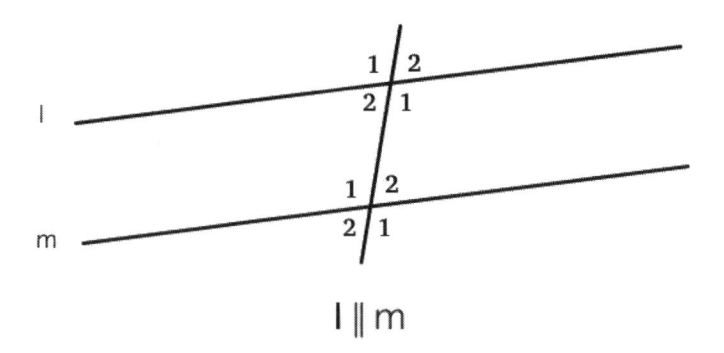

l ∥ m

All angles labeled 1 have the same angle measure, while all angles labeled 2 share the same angle measure. But have you thought about why this is?

I'm going to zoom in on one of the intersections of the figure above, and I want you to tell me if we are looking at line l or line m.

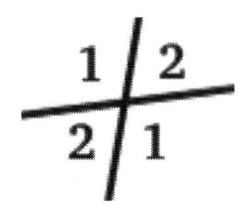

$$\frac{1 \mid 2}{2 \mid 1}$$

That's right! Because since they have the same slope and intersect with the vertical line in the same exact way, they're basically the same: you can't tell whether the horizontal line is line m or l. This is precisely the same reason why we can say every angle 1 has the same angle measure and every angle 2 as well.

Angle-Algebra

Some angle problems on the ACT are a mix in some algebra. We will call these questions, angle-algebra problems. Creative, I know.

There are a couple of things you must be aware of when solving these.

a) Straight lines have 180 degrees.

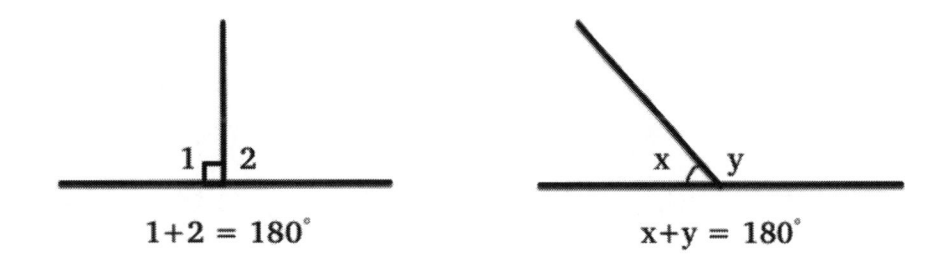

1+2 = 180°   x+y = 180°

b) The interior angles of any triangle add up to 180 degrees.

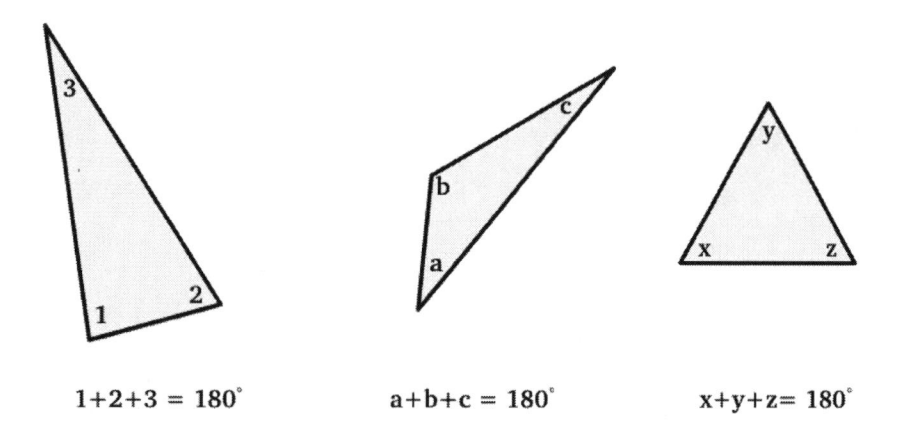

1+2+3 = 180°   a+b+c = 180°   x+y+z = 180°

c) The interior angles of any quadrilateral add up to 360 degrees.

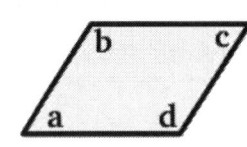

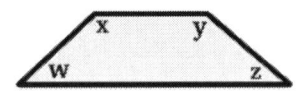

1+2+3+4 = 360°   a+b+c+d = 360°   w+x+y+z = 360°

d) The interior angles of an n-sided polygon adds up to (n-2)*180 degrees.

hexagon

(6-2)*180

4*180 = 720 degrees

octagon

(8-2)*180

6*180 = 1080 degrees

dodecagon

(12-2)*180

6*180 = 1800 degrees

e) To find the angle measure of each side in an n-sided regular polygon divide the total number of degrees (equation above) by n.

hexagon

720 /6 =

120 ° per angle

octagon

1080/8 =

135 ° per angle

dodecagon

1800/12 =

150 ° per angle

Let's use some of the above information to set up an algebra problem to solve the following problem.

Solve for the value of x

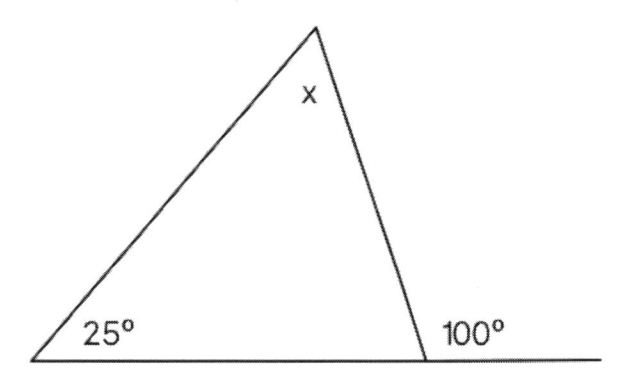

Since 100° is on the same line as the angle across from 25°, we know the two must add up to 180°.

Now that we know the 2nd angle is 80°, we can solve for x.

$$25+80+x=180$$
$$105+x=180$$

$$x=75$$

Practice Angle-Algebra Problems

1. Solve for y

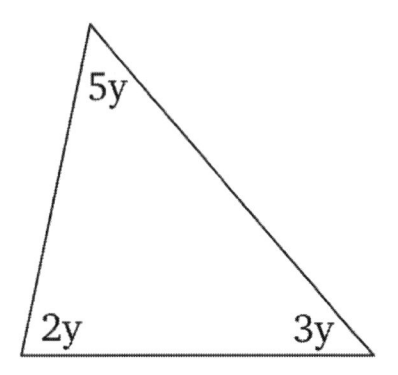

   (triangle with angles 5y, 2y, 3y)

2. Solve for x

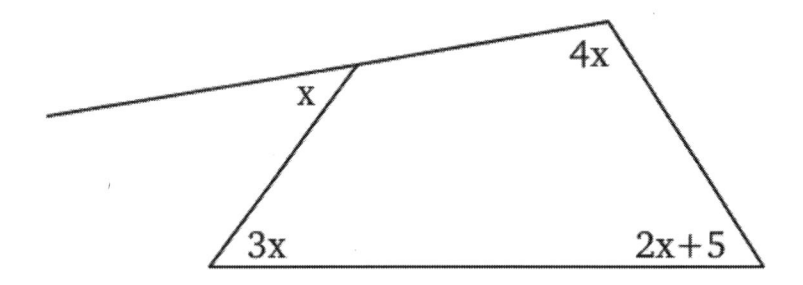

   (figure with angles x, 4x, 3x, 2x+5)

3. What is the value of the largest angle in the figure below?

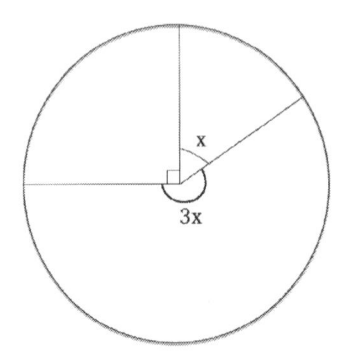

   (circle with central angles x, 3x, and a right angle)

Additional **Angles and Angle-Algebra** Questions in the *RACT Guide*

Test 1, page 173, # 40
Test 2, page 305, # 6
Test 2, page 307, # 17
Test 2, page 314, # 43
Test 3, page 458, # 35
Test 4, page 590, # 10

14. Triangles

Special Right Triangles

Do you remember your special right triangles from geometry class?

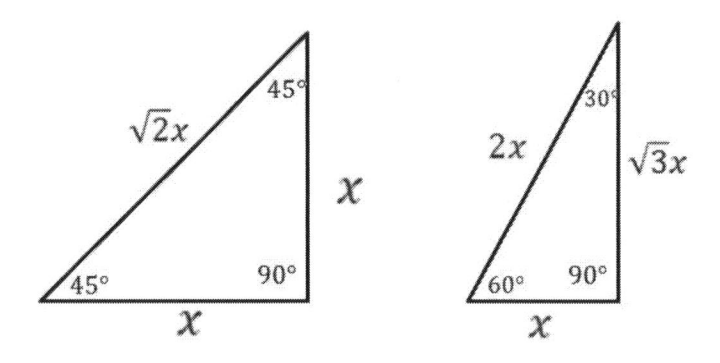

Memorize these triangles and the proportions of their side lengths. You will thank me later.

In any math problem, whenever you see a $\sqrt{2}$, $\sqrt{3}$, you should anticipate the question to deal with special right triangles!

Whenever you see $\sqrt{2}$, think 45-45-90.
Whenever you see $\sqrt{3}$, think 30-60-90.

Of course, it's not always so straightforward. The ACT won't always just give you a triangle and label the angles for you. Sometimes these triangles are a little more camouflaged. 30-60-90 triangles can be hidden in an equilateral triangle split right down the middle, while 45-45-90 triangles can be hidden in a square split diagonally.

Split an equilateral triangle and it becomes two 30-60-90 triangles

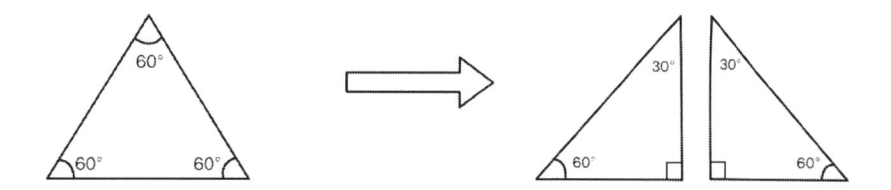

Split a square and it becomes two 45-45-90 triangles

Common Right Triangles

These are the lengths of the sides of commonly used triangles on the ACT. Memorizing these allows you to instantly solve some triangle problems you might have had to do the Pythagorean Theorem for. And remember, the longest side of any triangle is always the hypotenuse.

Since these are right triangles, this also means that triangles similar to these are also right triangles, meaning multiples of these side lengths will also give you right triangles.

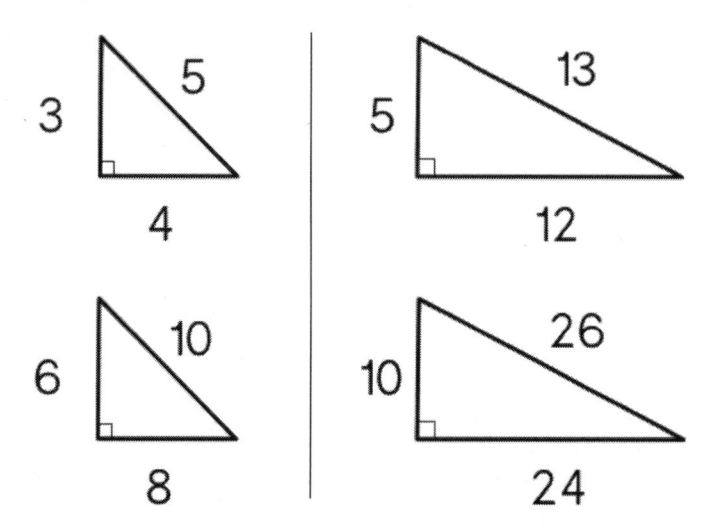

Similar Triangles

Let's get wacky. If I were to take a shrink ray and shrink you down, you would become a mini-me version of your normal-sized self. Although you would be smaller, your body would still be proportionately the same. If before the shrinkage, your legs were half as long as your arms, they would still be half as long now. If your pinky was twice as long as your thumb, this would also not change.

This is exactly the case with similar triangles: two triangles, one regular-sized triangle and a mini, but still proportionate, version of that triangle. These triangles are "similar" to one another.

In order for us to define two triangles as similar, all 3 angles need to be the same in each triangle. However, if we find that two angles are the same that must mean the third angle is also the same.

When solving a problem that deals with similar triangles, we just need to set up a proportion to solve for the unknown side.

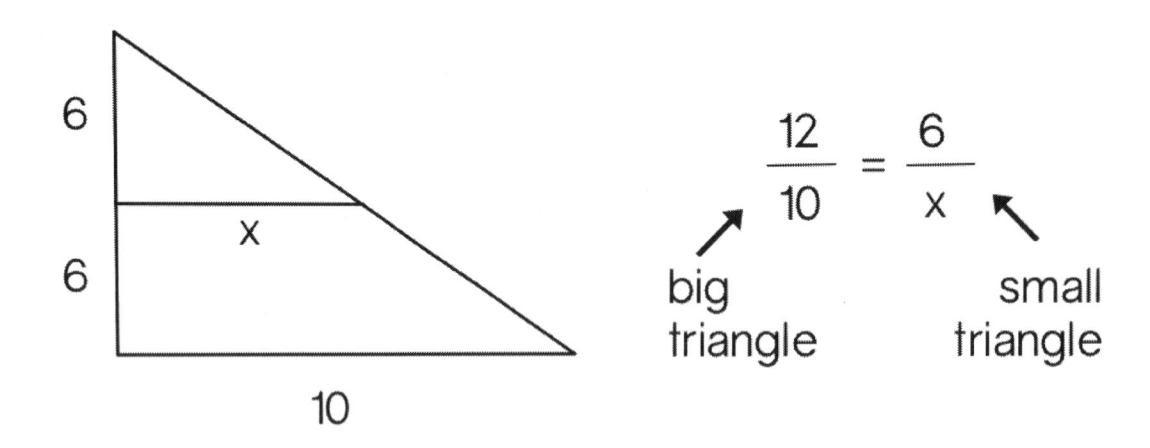

$$\frac{12}{10} = \frac{6}{x}$$

↗ big triangle   ↖ small triangle

Then, just like whenever we have fractions on opposite sides of an equals sign, we cross multiply.

$$12x = 60$$
$$x = 5$$

Rotate Those Triangles

Sometimes the ACT likes to rotate similar triangles and make it easy for students to set the wrong sides as proportionate to one another. In this case, redraw the triangles in the same direction to avoid making this mistake.

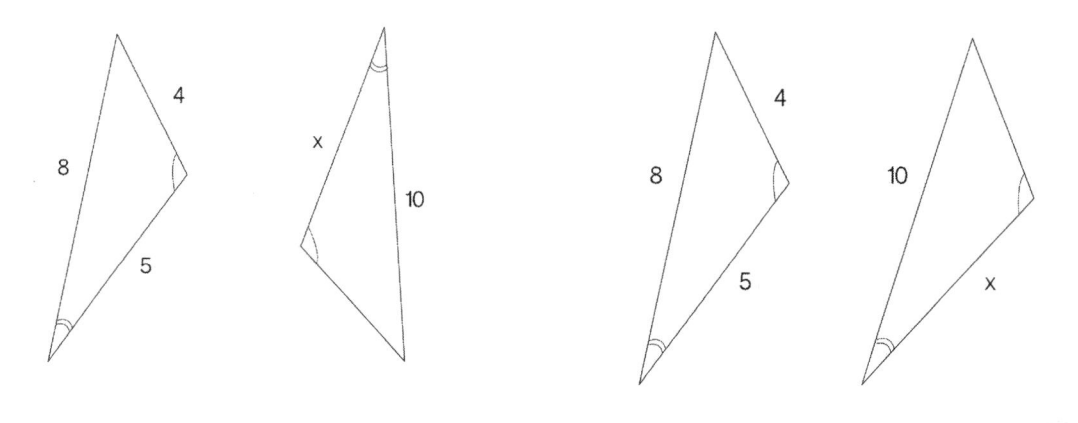

EASY TO MAKE A MISTAKE   HARD TO MAKE A MISTAKE

Triangle Inequality Theorem

While it sounds fancy, it simply means *the sum of any two sides of a triangle must be greater than the third.*

To help demonstrate this theorem, let's consider the following two triangles with the following side lengths: 3,4,5 and 2,3,5.

Can 3,4, and 5 be the sides of a triangle?

$$3+4 = 7 \qquad 7 > 5$$
$$4+5 = 9 \qquad 9 > 3$$
$$3+5 = 8 \qquad 8 > 4$$

Yes. The sum of any 2 sides are greater than the third.

Can 2, 3, and 5 be the side lengths of a triangle?

$$3+5 = 8 \qquad 8 > 2$$
$$2+5 = 7 \qquad 7 > 3$$
$$2+3 = 5 \qquad 5 \not> 5$$

No. Not all sums of 2 sides are greater than the third.

Conclusion: while 3, 4, and 5 can be sides of a triangle, 2, 3, and 5 cannot.

Triangles: *In Summary*

Special Right Triangles

- Memorize the side proportions of your 45-45-90 and 30-60-90 triangles
- When you see $\sqrt{2}$ in a problem, think 45-45-90
- When you see $\sqrt{3}$ in a problem think 30-60-90
- A diagonally-split square results in two 45-45-90 triangles
- A split equilateral triangle results in two 30-60-90 triangles

Common Right Triangles

- Right triangles with sides 3-4-5 and 5-12-13 are common on the ACT
- Triangles with multiples of these sides are also right triangles

    3-4-5   ———-> 6-8-10 and 12-16-20
    5-12-13   ———-> 10-24-26 and 20-48-52

Similar Right Triangles

- You need two equal angles to know that two triangles are similar
- Rotate and align similar triangles before you set the proportion

Triangle Inequality Theorem

- The sum of any two sides of a triangle must be greater than the third
- If it doesn't meet this rule, it's not a triangle

Practice **Triangles** Problems

1. In the triangle below AB = 6, BD = 8, and CE = 24. What is the length of segment DE?

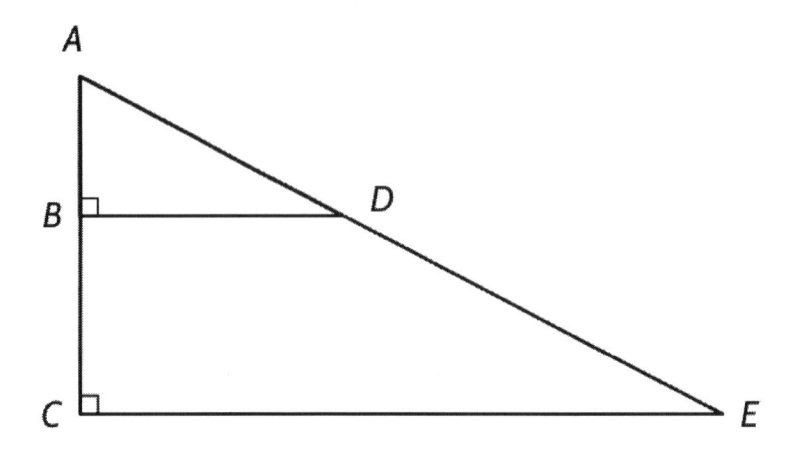

Figure is NOT drawn to scale.

2. Two sides of a triangle are 7 and 11. List all possible values for the third side.

3. A square with a side length of 6 is inscribed within a circle as shown below. What is the area of the circle?

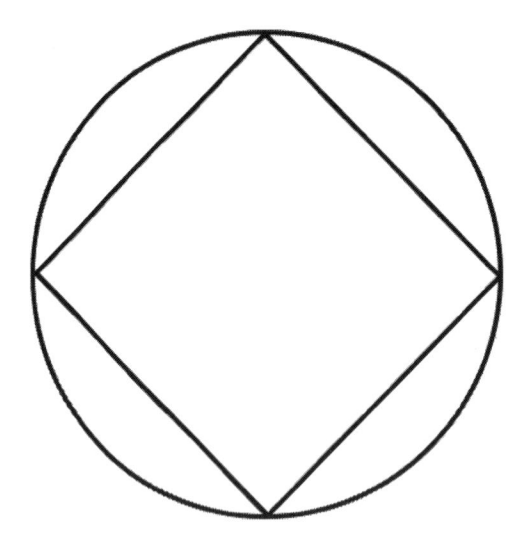

Additional **Triangles** Questions in the *RACT Guide*

Test 1, page 168, # 20
Test 1, page 169, # 25
Test 2, page 305, # 7
Test 2, page 306, # 14
Test 2, page 307, # 15
Test 2, page 310, # 31
Test 2, page 315, # 48
Test 2, page 216, # 52
Test 2, page 305, # 7
Test 3, page 450, # 4
Test 3, page 451, # 8
Test 3, page 457, # 30

Test 3, page 459, # 41
Test 4, page 588, # 1
Test 4, page 590, # 10
Test 4, page 591, # 15
Test 4, page 592, # 20
Test 4, page 598, # 44
Test 4, page 598, # 45
Test 5, page 739, # 30
Test 5, page 739, # 33
Test 5, page 741, # 38
Test 5, page 746, # 58

15. Circles

Central Angles, Sector Areas, and Arc Lengths

If I gave you a circle with an area of 100 and asked you to find the area of a sector with a central angle of 180°, what might you answer me?

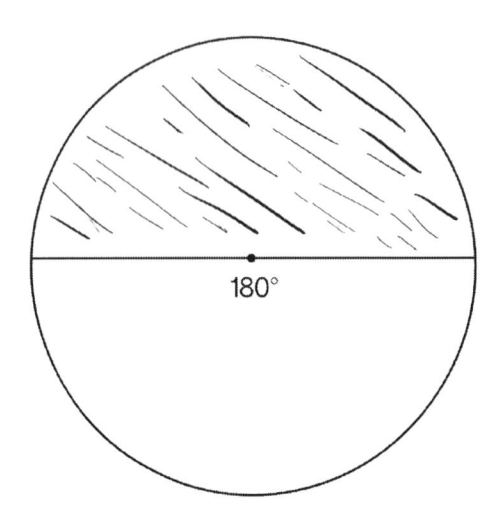

If area of circle=100
What is area of the shaded sector?

Since 180° is half of a circle's 360 degrees, you'd be correct to guess that the sector's area would be half of the circle's area, or 50.

Circle area = 100

180 is half of 360

Sector Area must be half of 100, or 50

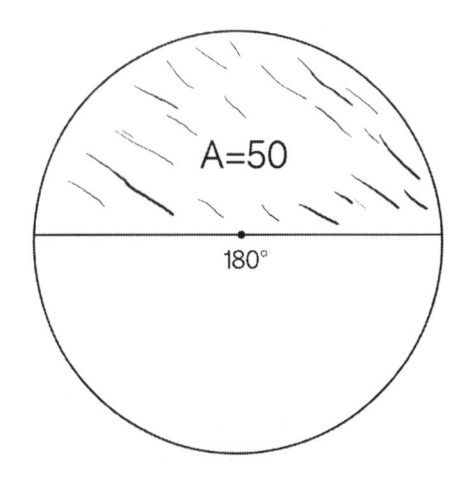

What if I asked you to find the area of a 90 degree sector of that same circle? How would the problem change?

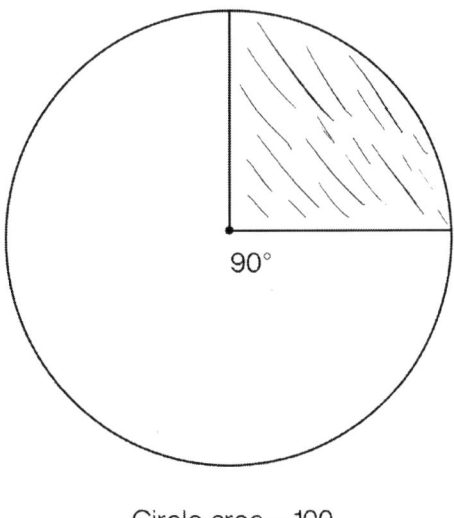

Circle area = 100

What is the area of the shaded sector?

The same logic applies here. Since 90° is a quarter of a circle's 360 degrees, the sector's area would also be one quarter of the circle's area, or 25.

Circle area = 100

90 is one fourth of 360

Sector Area is one fourth of 100 or **25**

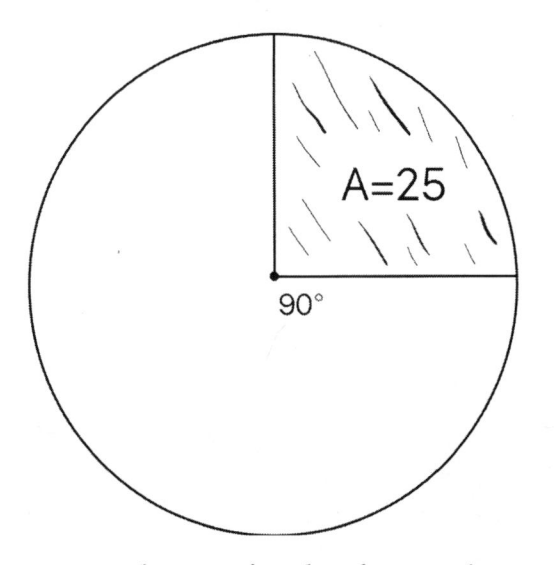

So, by using the same logic, if we had a sector with a central angle of 120°, one third of 360°, the area of the sector will be one third the circle's area.

This concept works the same way with arc lengths.

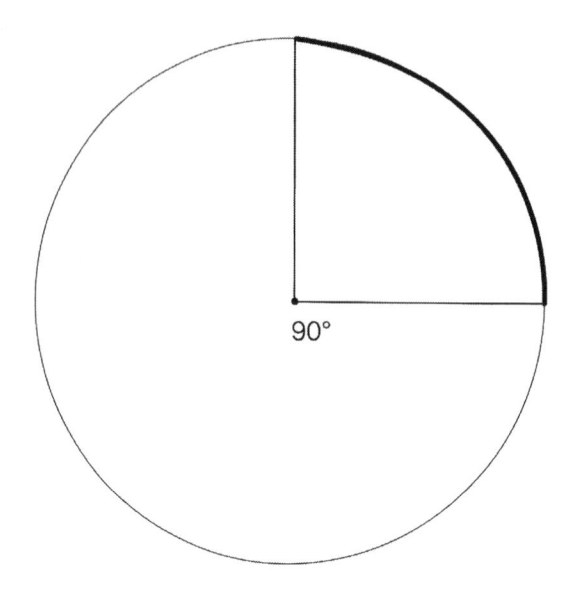

90°

Total Circumference = 40

Arc Length of 90° sector = 10

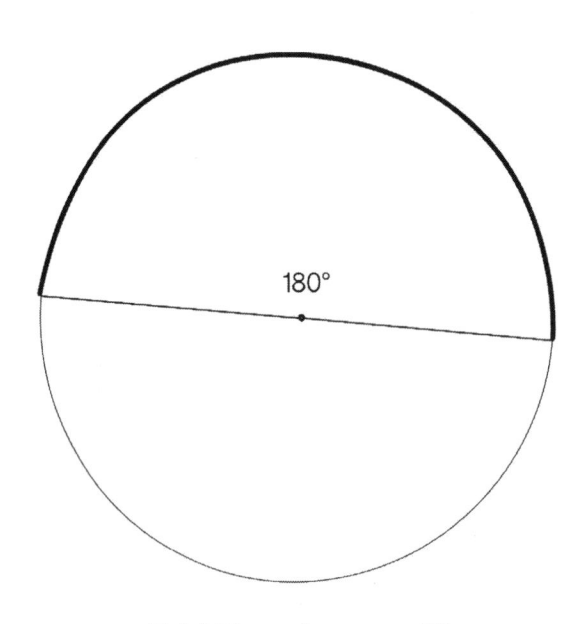

180°

Total Circumference = 50

Arc Length of 180° sector = 25

What all this means is that **both the area and the arc length of a sector are directly proportional to the relationship of the sector angle to 360.** In other words, it's all about ratios!

When faced with a problem like this, you can use the following equations to find your unknown variable, whatever it may be.

SECTOR AREA AND ARC LENGTH EQUATIONS

$$\frac{\text{degrees of central angle}}{360} = \frac{\text{area of sector}}{\text{total area of circle}}$$

$$\frac{\text{degrees of central angle}}{360} = \frac{\text{arc length of sector}}{\text{total circumference of circle}}$$

Now, let's do some examples together using some numbers that aren't so neat and tidy.

Example 1

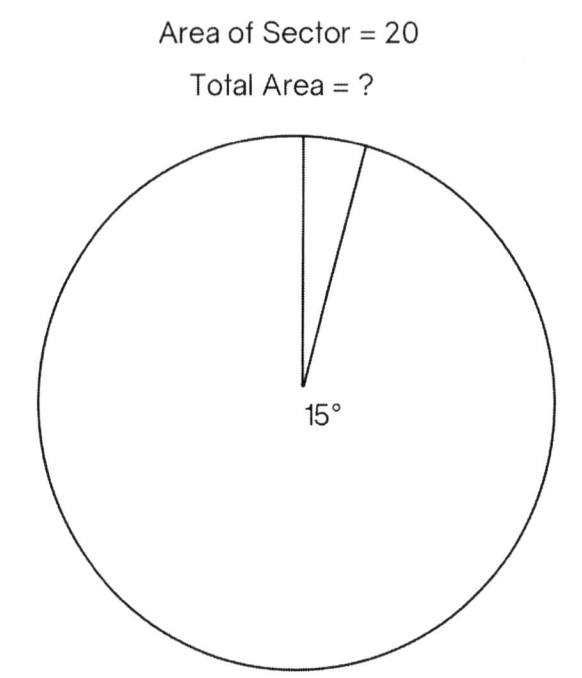

Area of Sector = 20

Total Area = ?

15°

First, we set up our proportion.

$$\frac{15}{360} = \frac{20}{\text{total area}}$$

Then, as with any proportion problem we cross-multiply…

15(total area) = 7200

total area = 480

Not so bad after all…

Example 2

Circumference = 60

Sector Arc Length = ?

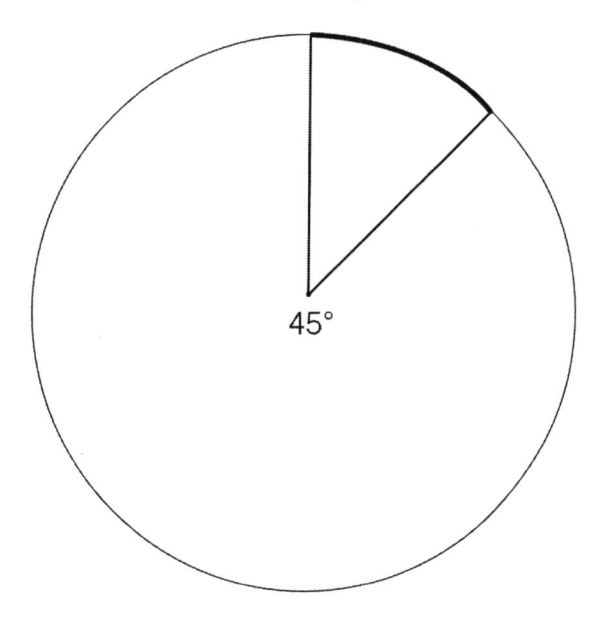

$$\frac{45}{360} = \frac{\text{arc length}}{60}$$

2700 = arc length (360)

arc length = 7.5

Things are getting a little clearer, right?

Example 3

Sector Area = 60

Radius = 10

Central angle of Sector = ?

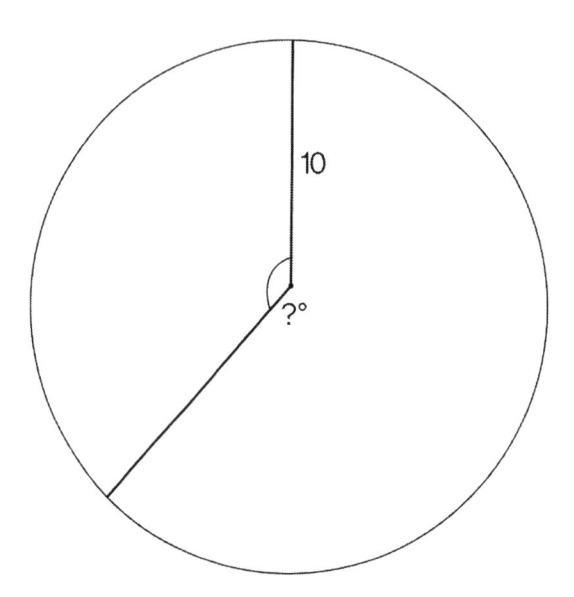

Figure Not Drawn to Scale

First, we have to find the total area using the radius we were given.

$$A = \pi(10)^2 \qquad A = 100\pi$$

Now we can set up our proportion.

$$\frac{\text{sector angle}}{360} = \frac{60}{100\pi}$$

21600 = 314.2 (sector angle)

68.8° = sector angle

I knew you had it in you!

Circles: *In Summary*

- To find the arc length, circumference, central sector angle, or circle area you can use the following two equations:

$$\frac{\text{degrees of central angle}}{360} = \frac{\text{area of sector}}{\text{total area of circle}}$$

$$\frac{\text{degrees of central angle}}{360} = \frac{\text{arc length of sector}}{\text{total circumference of circle}}$$

- Sometimes with these problems, you will need to use the radius to find the circumference or area and then find your unknown.

Practice **Circle** Problems

1. The area of sector B is 15 and the central angle of the sector is 18°. What is the total area of the circle?

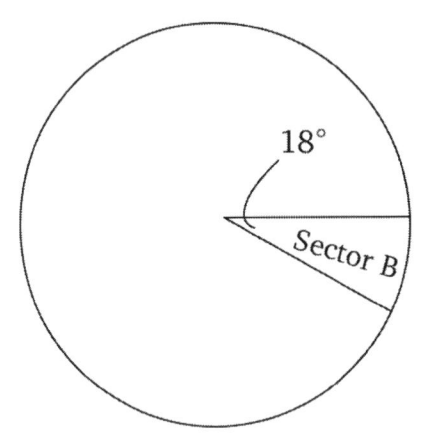

2. Lauren makes a pie chart of how many pairs of shoes she has. If the sector for high heels has a central angle that measures 72°, and she has 400 shoes in total, how many high heels does Lauren have in her collection?

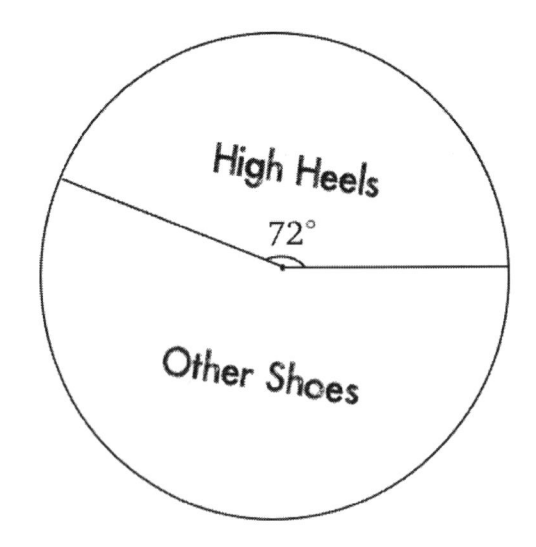

3. The diameter of the Big Ben clock face in London is 23 feet. How many feet does the outer edge of the minute hand travel from 1 PM to 1:25 PM?

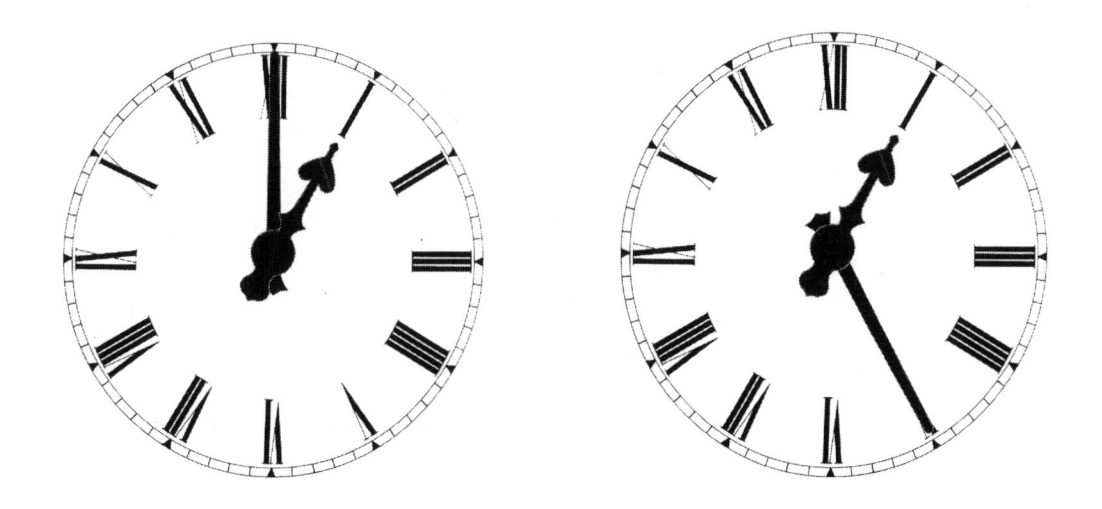

Additional **Circles** Questions in the *RACT Guide*

Test 1, page 175, # 46
Test 3, page 460, # 43
Test 4, page 595, # 34

16. The Circle Equation

This equation is on your equations sheet in the beginning of this section, but I want to put a special emphasis on it here. On most ACT tests, there is at least one question if not two involving the circle equation. These questions are basically free points, but you have to have the equation memorized in order to get those points.

The equation of a circle with the center coordinates (h,k) and radius r is

$$(x-h)^2+(y-k) = r^2$$

So a circle that has a center of (4,3) with a radius of 3 will have the equation

$$(x-4)^2+(y-3)^2 = 9$$

On a coordinate plane this equation would graph as so:

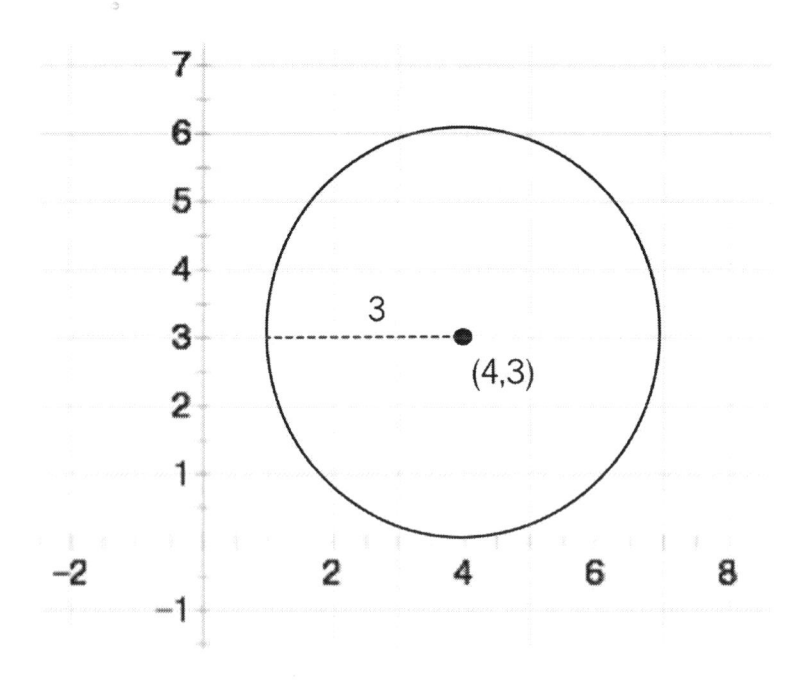

The Circle Equation: *In Summary*

- On most ACT's, there is at least one question that requires the knowledge of the graphing equation of a circle.

- These are easy points as long as you have the equation memorized.

- The equation of a circle with the center coordinates (h,k) and radius r is:

$$(x-h)^2 + (y-k) = r^2$$

Practice **The Circle Equation** Problems

1. Write the equation for a circle with a radius of 4 and center coordinates of (6,-10).

2. Write the equation for a circle with a radius of 6 and center coordinates of (-4,-5).

3. A circle tangent to the x-axis at 3 has center coordinates of (3,-5). What is the equation for this circle?

Additional **The Circle Equation** Questions in the *RACT Guide*

Test 1, page 175, # 47
Test 4, page 599, # 46
Test 5, page 735, # 15

17. SOH-CAH-TOA

Haven't taken trig yet? Took trig but detested it? Have no fear!

The ACT covers trigonometry but only very sparsely: around four to five questions on each 60-question Math section. Not to mention that most of these questions cover SOH-CAH-TOA, which is easy to master.

For those of you who are new to trig or need a little refresher, voila. For those who are already familiar with it, you can skip this part.

For every triangle trig problem, you have your angle, the side opposite the angle (O), the side adjacent the angle (A), and the hypotenuse (H).

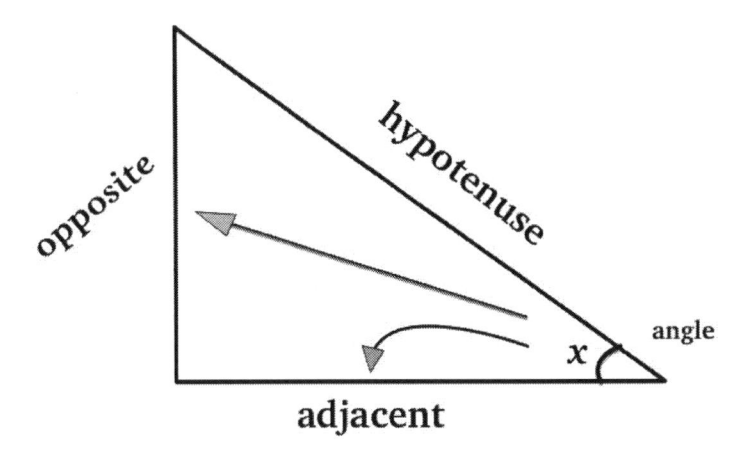

SOH-CAH-TOA is simply an acronym of the side ratios that correspond to each trig function.

Sine

$Sin(x) = O/H$

Cosine

$Cos(x) = A/H$

Tangent

$Tan(x) = O/A$

These trig functions also have inverses that are important to know as well.

Cosecant (inverse of Sine)
Csc(x) = H/O

Secant (inverse of cosine)
Cos (x) = H/A

Cotangent (inverse of tangent)
Cot (x) = A/O

SOH-CAH-TOA problems are essentially all the same, once you break them down. There are always three variables: angle measure, the length of the first side (a, o, or h), and the length of the second side (also a, o, or h). Of these three variables, there are always two that are known and one that is unknown. It is your job to solve for that unknown variable.

Your unknown is either one of the sides of the triangle...

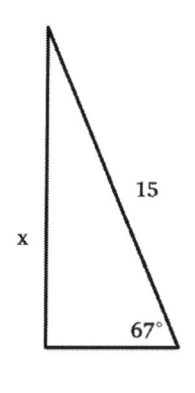

Sin (67) = o/15

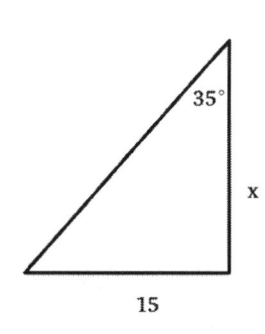

Tan (35) = 15/a

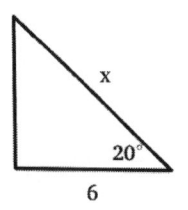

Cos (20) = 6/h

...or your unknown is your angle

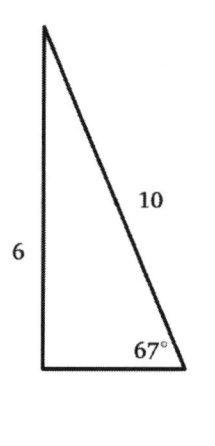

Sin (x) = 6/10

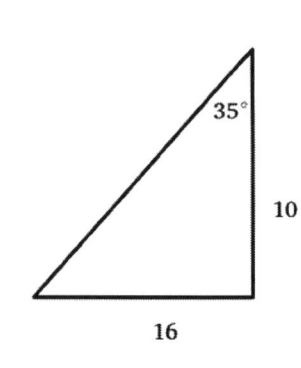

Tan (x) = 16/10

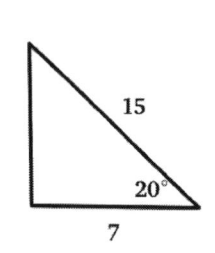

Cos (x) = 7/15

These problems are simple once you realize that all of these problems are essentially the same for one reason: *there is one unknown variable you have to solve for.*

If the Unknown is Your Angle, Use Sin^{-1}, Cos^{-1}, Tan^{-1}

In the case that your unknown is your angle, you will have to use the inverse trig functions in your calculator.

For example, if you're solving for angle x, your opposite side is 20, and your hypotenuse side is 15, you would enter "Sin^{-1}(20/15)" into your calculator, and the answer you receive will be the measure of angle x.

THE GOLDEN SOH-CAH-TOA PROCESS

Whenever dealing with a SOH-CAH-TOA problem, taking the following steps can help you always get the right answer.

1) Identify the angle in question

2) Label your opposite, adjacent, and hypotenuse sides on the triangle

3) Fill in your variables into your equation, leaving all except the unknown.

4) Solve for your unknown.

See? I told you it wasn't so bad. You're well on your way to becoming a SOH-CAH-TOA Jedi.

SOH-CAH-TOA: *In Summary*

- There are only four to five trig questions on the ACT.

- Most of these questions are SOH-CAH-TOA.

- To easily solve SOH-CAH-TOA problems…

    1) Identify the angle in question.

    2) Label your opposite, adjacent, and hypotenuse sides on the triangle.

    3) Fill in your variables into your equation, leaving all except the unknown.

    4) Solve for your unknown.

Trig Functions	Inverses of Trig Functions	More Useful Info
$\sin(x) = o/h$	$\text{Cosecant}(x) = h/o$	$\sin(x)/\cos(x) = \tan(x)$
$\cos(x) = a/h$	$\text{Secant}(x) = h/a$	
$\tan(x) = o/a$	$\text{Cotangent}(x) = a/o$	

Practice SOH-CAH-TOA Problems

1. Name the inverse of each trig function.

a) cos
b) tan
c) sin

2. Using the triangle below, find cos∠B ?

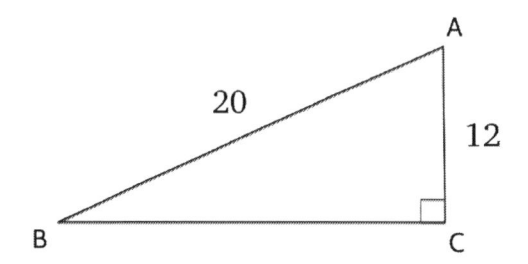

3. A completely vertical flagpole that is 20 feet tall casts a shadow on the ground. A string is tied to the tip of the flagpole and the other end of the string is brought down to the tip of the shadow. The angle of the string with the ground is 35°. What is the length of the shadow?

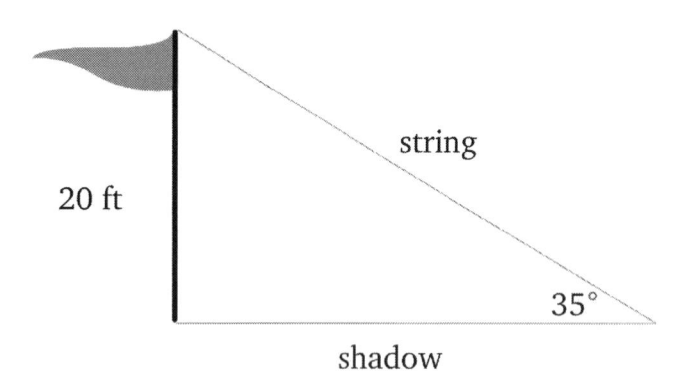

Additional **SOH-CAH-TOA** Questions in the *RACT Guide*

Test 1, page 169, # 24
Test 1, page 170, # 28
Test 2, page 308, # 20
Test 2, page 314, # 45
Test 3, page 461, # 46
Test 4, page 596, # 37
Test 4, page 601, # 54
Test 5, page 743, # 46
Test 5, page 746, # 58

18. Other Trig Stuff

The majority of ACT trigonometry questions tests basic SOH-CAH-TOA knowledge, but for that small minority of other trig question types, here is a small reference section for math-inclined students.

For those of you trying to get over a 30 on the math, this information is important. However, for those of you who are aiming around the mid 20's, your time might be best spent elsewhere.

The Unit Circle

For the interest of time and because there are usually two or fewer unit circle problems on the ACT, I won't be going into too much depth about the unit circle.

The primary purpose of the unit circle is to draw SOH-CAH-TOA triangles. The two things we need to know is where we will draw our triangles and how we draw the triangles.

Where We Draw Our Triangles

To draw these SOH-CAH-TOA triangles, we use a special xy-coordinate plane just like what we would use to graph any other function, but here it's a little different.

Each of the four corners of the xy-axis is labeled with a radian value to help mark in which quadrant we will draw our triangle. We start with "0" at the beginning of quadrant I and move counter-clockwise, increasing by increments of π/2 and ending at 2π after one full rotation. This circular progression is why we call this the unit **circle**.

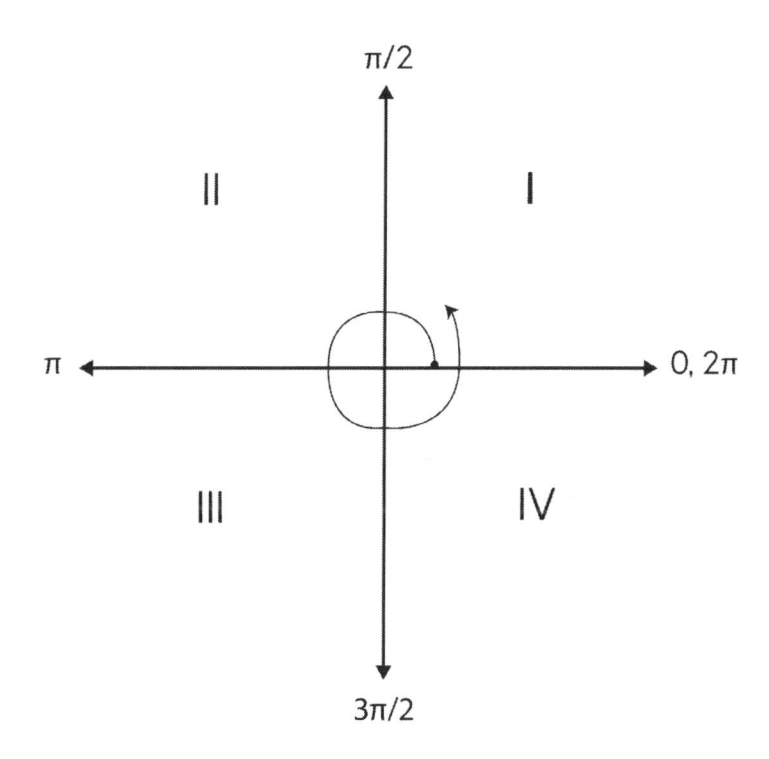

The symbol Θ represents the central angle of the triangle

If   0 < Θ < π/2   draw your triangle in quadrant 1.
If   π/2 < Θ < π   draw your triangle in quadrant 2.
If   π < Θ < 3π/2   draw your triangle in quadrant 3.
If   3π/2 < Θ < 2π   draw your triangle in quadrant 4.

How We Draw These Triangles

As I stated before, the only purpose of the unit circle is to make triangles. Let's now do just that.

First, always draw your hypotenuse from the origin. The triangle in this example is located in quadrant I, between 0 and π/2.

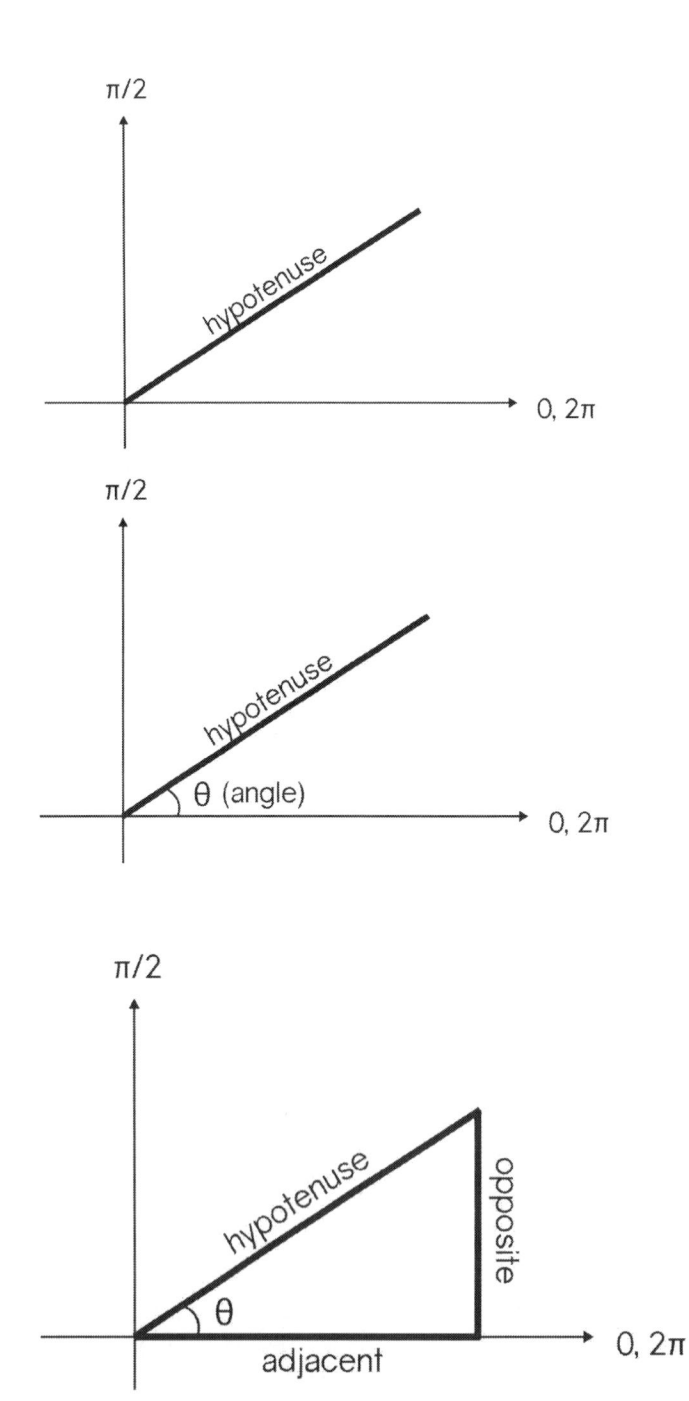

Now, since this triangle was in quadrant I, and the x and y values are positive, both the opposite and adjacent sides are positive. However, if we were to move this triangle to another quadrant we might have some different results.

While the hypotenuse of a triangle in any quadrant is always positive…

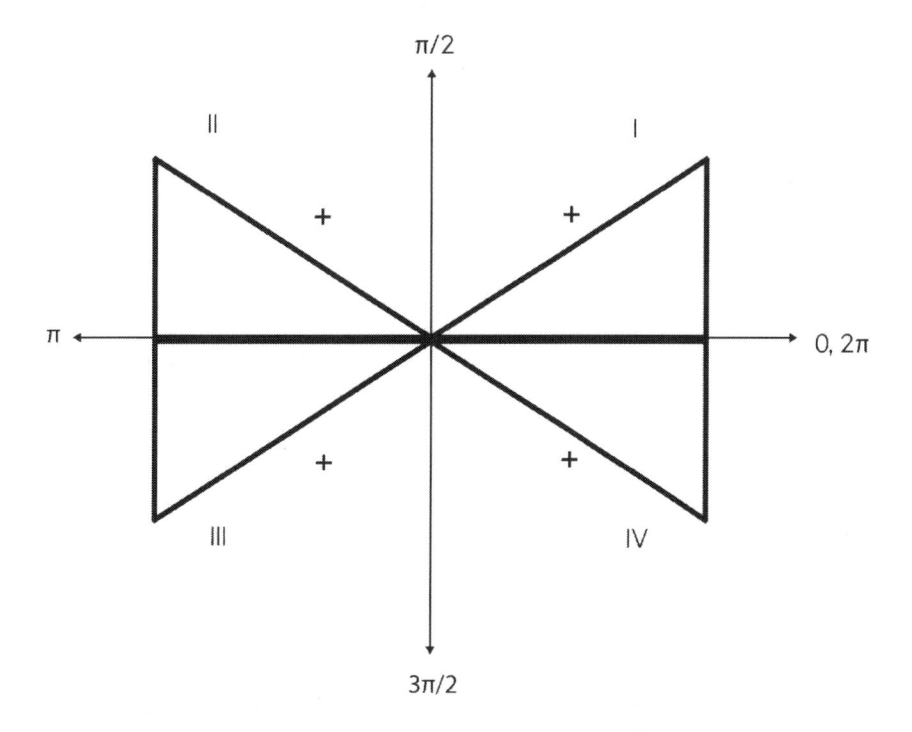

the same is not true for the legs of the triangle

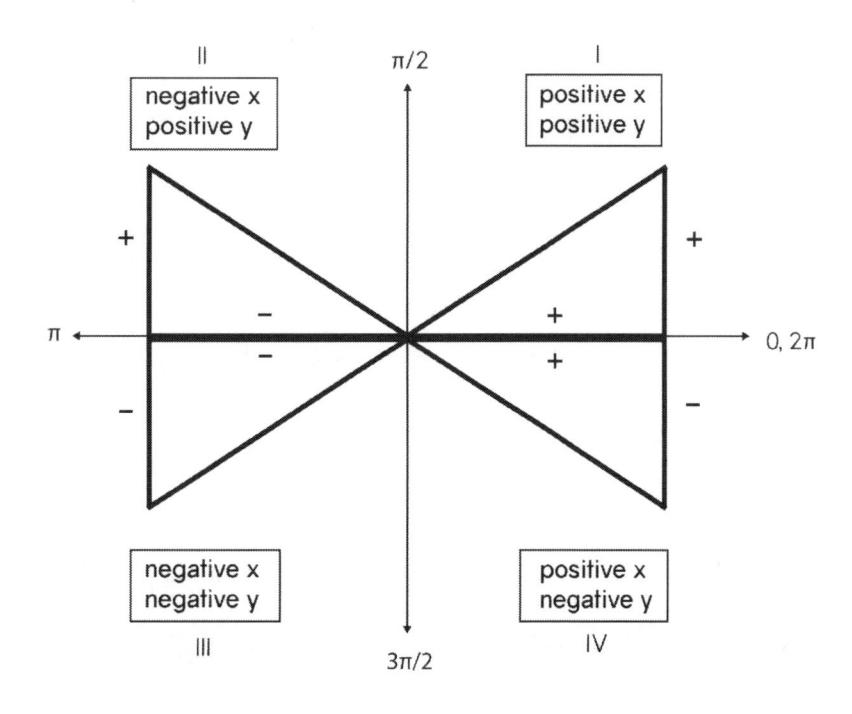

So if I were to draw a triangle with side lengths 6,8 and 10 on the unit circle, the signs of the legs (6 and 8) would change depending on which quadrant it was in.

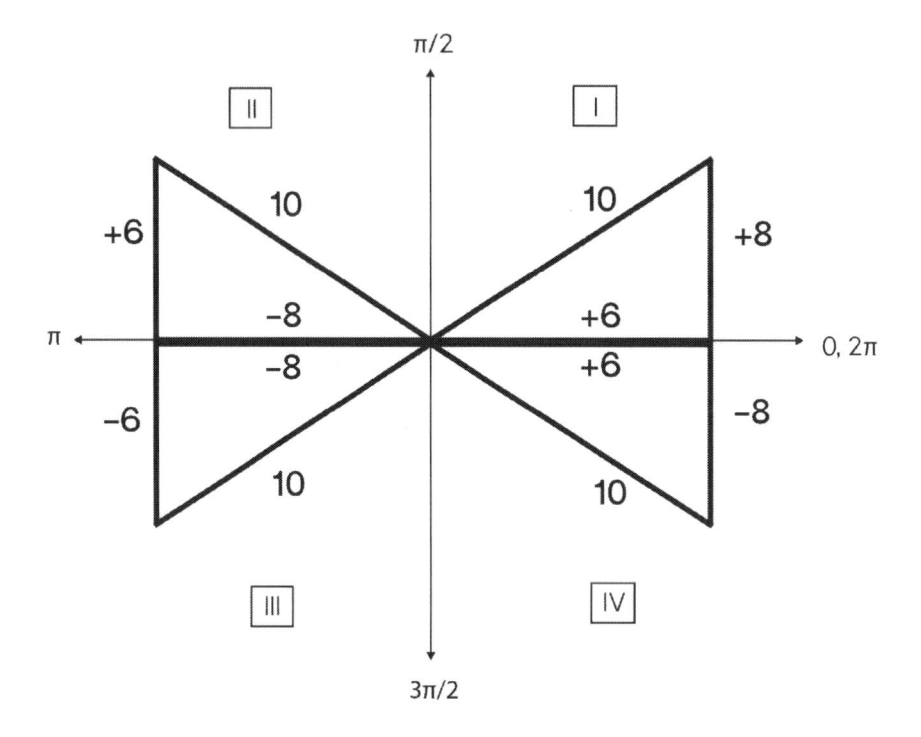

Because the quadrant will change the sign of the legs, this will affect the values we get for sine, cosine, and tangent (SOH-CAH-TOA).

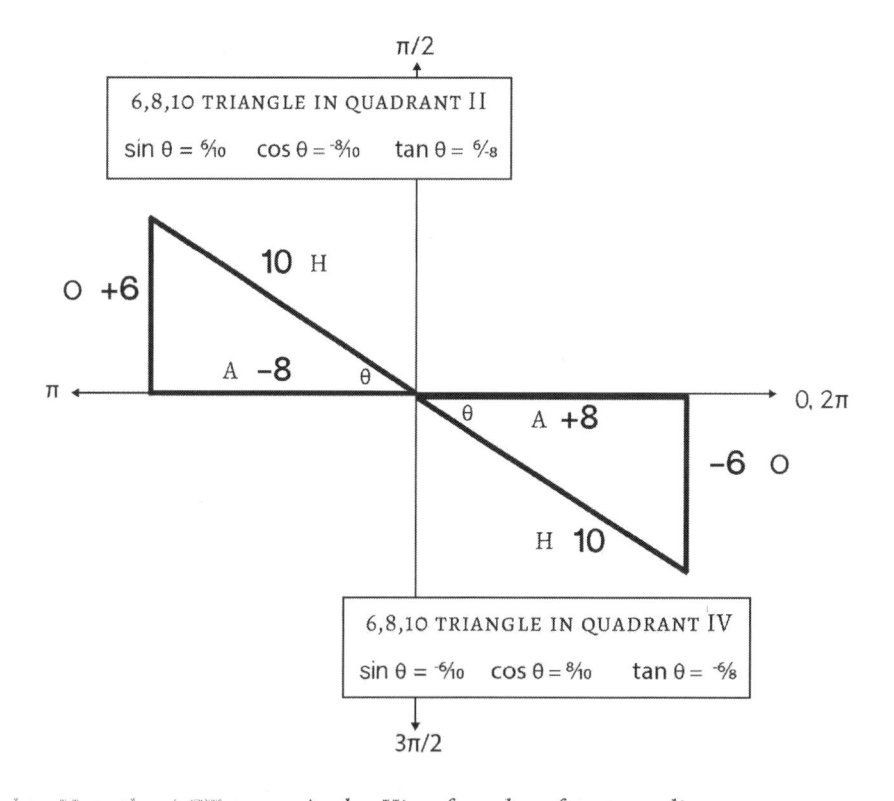

6,8,10 TRIANGLE IN QUADRANT II
$\sin \theta = 6/10$ $\cos \theta = -8/10$ $\tan \theta = 6/-8$

6,8,10 TRIANGLE IN QUADRANT IV
$\sin \theta = -6/10$ $\cos \theta = 8/10$ $\tan \theta = -6/8$

6,8,10 TRIANGLE IN QUADRANT I

sin θ = 6/10   cos θ = 8/10   tan θ = 6/8

6,8,10 TRIANGLE IN QUADRANT III

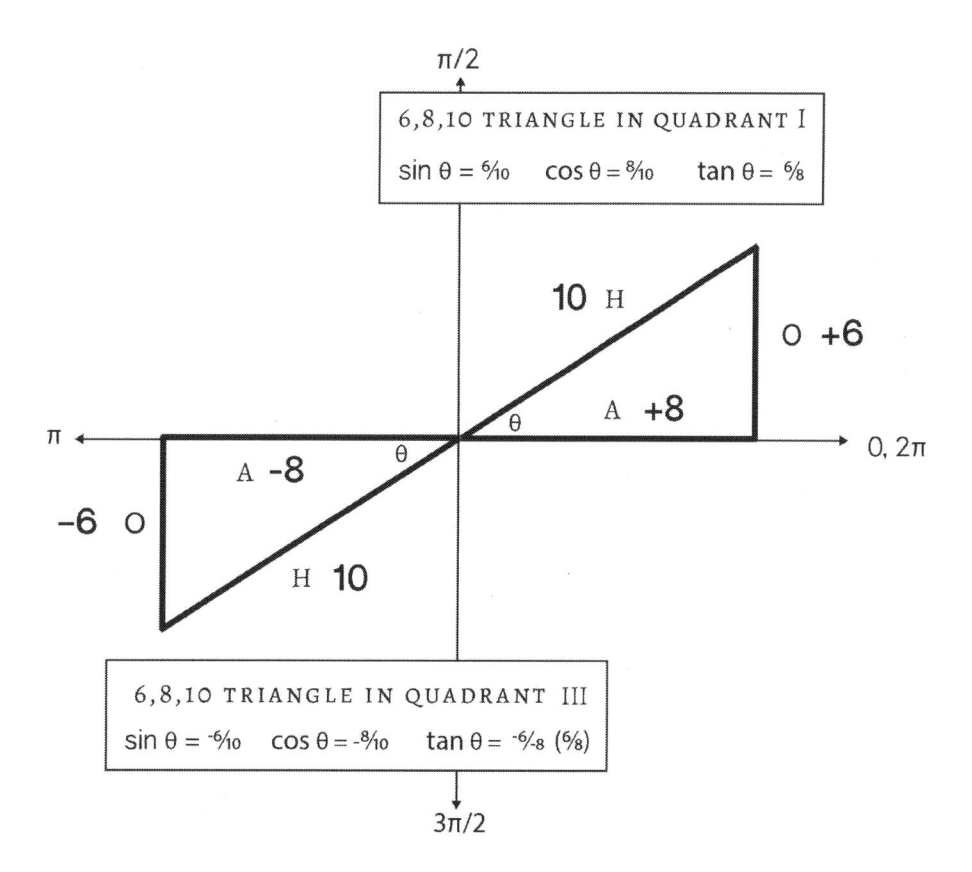

sin θ = -6/10   cos θ = -8/10   tan θ = -6/-8 (6/8)

Let's do a sample problem together:

Draw the triangle represented by tangent θ = -12/9 in one of its possible quadrants. Then find sin θ.

Well, since the tangent value given to us is negative, the triangle can't be located in quadrant I or III, both of which have positive values for tangent. It must be located in quadrant II or IV.

Here is what the triangle looks like in quadrant II.

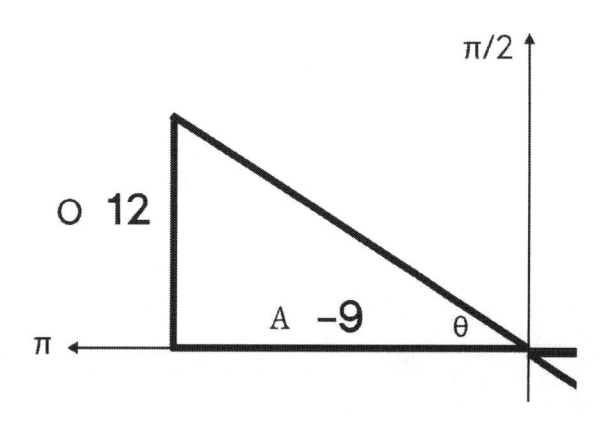

Using the Pythagorean Theorem we can find that the hypotenuse is 15.

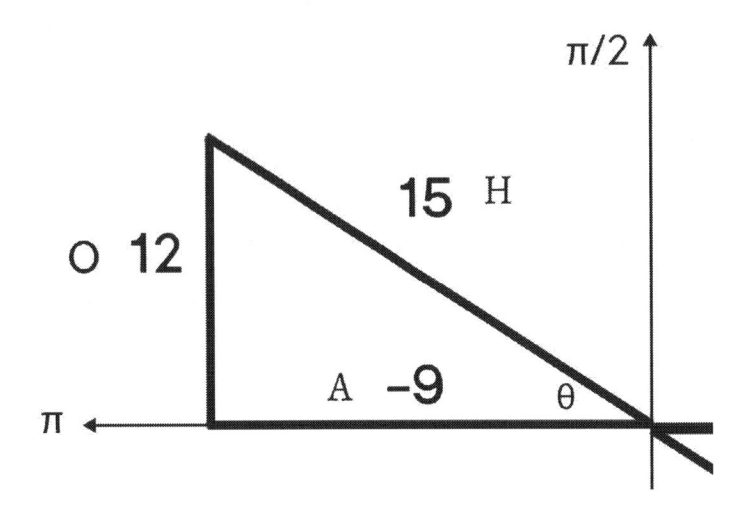

Sin θ *(or O/H)* must be 12/15 when θ is in quadrant II.

Amplitude

If a question asks you for the amplitude of a function, it's simply asking for how high the function peaks and how low it dips. The amplitude will always be a positive number, and in the example below it is 2.

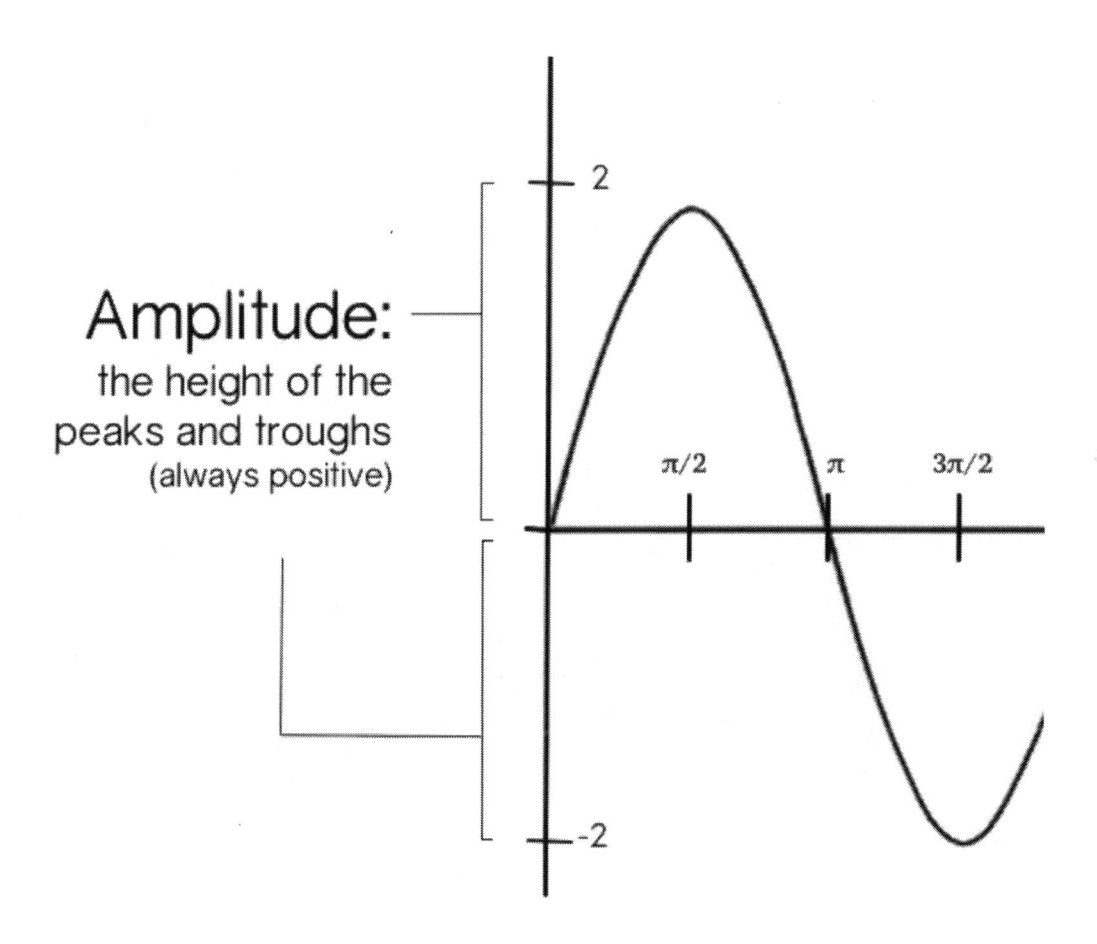

Amplitude: the height of the peaks and troughs (always positive)

Period

Sometimes on the ACT math you're given a graphed trig function and asked to find the period. But what is the period anyway?

The period is the distance required for the function to complete one full cycle. To put it in a simpler way, a period of a graphed trig function is the distance from peak to peak or trough to trough.

$5\pi/2 - \pi/2 = 2\pi$

period (peak to peak)

$\pi/2$ π $3\pi/2$ 2π $5\pi/2$ 3π $7\pi/2$ 4π

period (trough to trough)
$7\pi/2 - 3\pi/2 = 2\pi$

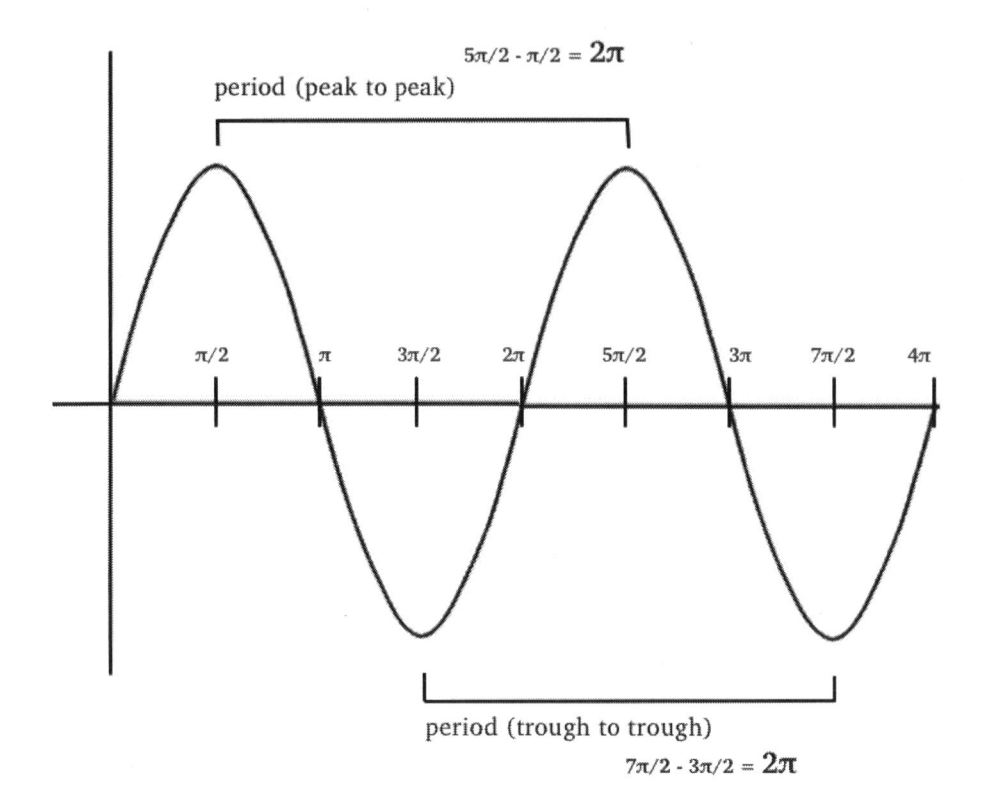

Notice how, in the above example, it does not matter if you find the distance between neighboring peaks or neighboring troughs. You still get the same value for the period: 2π.

Converting Radians to Degrees

Radians and degrees are two units used in math. Sometimes, albeit rarely, the ACT Math test has a question that gauges whether or not you can convert one to the other.

> Since $\pi = 180°$…
>
> To convert radians to degrees **multiply by $180/\pi$**
> To convert degrees to radians **multiply by $\pi/180$**

Just like in chemistry or physics, when you are converting units you always want to make sure your desired final unit is on top, in the numerator.

Other Trig Stuff: *In Summary*

Unit Circle

- The unit circle is used to draw SOH-CAH-TOA triangles

- We always draw the hypotenuse of a triangle from the origin

- Θ = the central angle the triangle makes with the origin

- Quadrant markers (0, π/2, π, 3π/2, 2π) will tell you in which quadrant you must draw your triangle

- Quadrants are important because they will tell you if the legs of your triangle are positive or negative

- The hypotenuse of any unit circle triangle is always positive

Amplitude

- Amplitude is the **height** of the peak or the trough of a wave function

Period

- The **length** of one complete cycle of a wave function

- Also known as the **distance** between peak to peak or trough to trough

Converting Degrees and Radians

- To go from radians to degrees - **Multiply by 180/π**

- To go from degrees to radians - **Multiply by π/180**

Practice **Other Trig Stuff** Questions

1. If $\pi/2 < \theta < \pi$, and $\cos \theta = -4/5$, what is $\sin \theta$?

2. What is the period and amplitude of the function below?

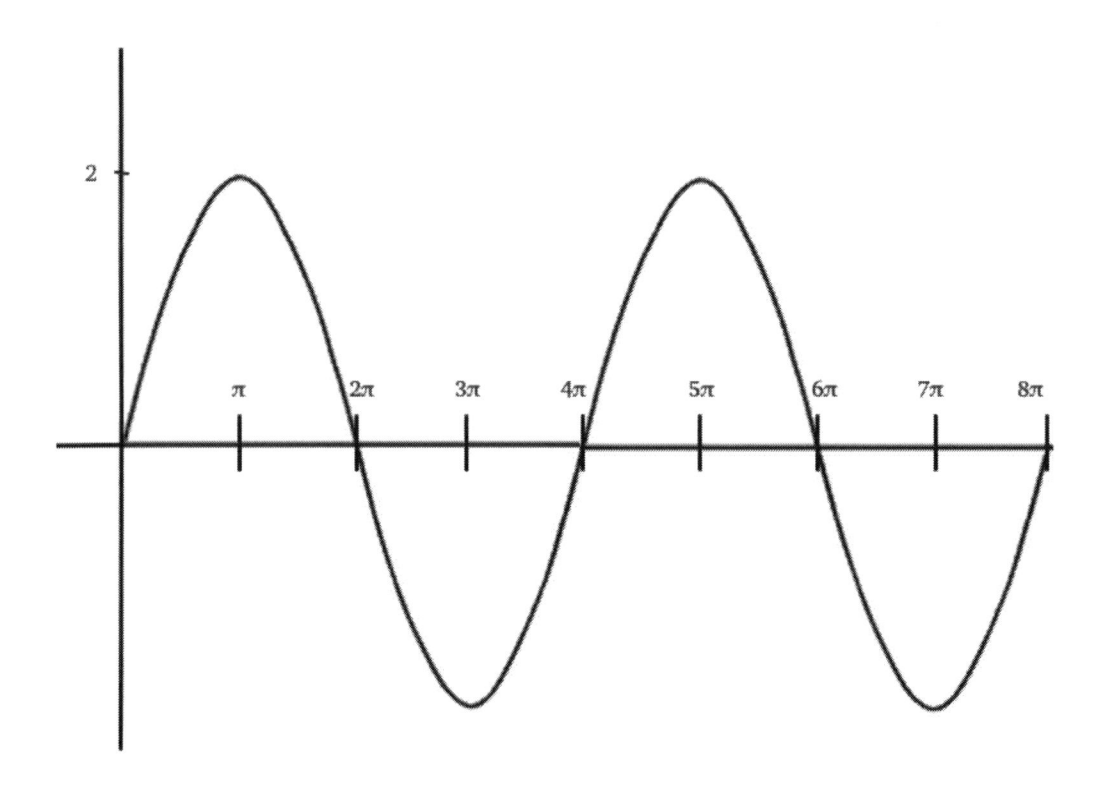

3. What is the period of sin 3x? (hint: use your graphing calculator!)

4. Convert 270 degrees to radians.

Additional **Other Trig Stuff** Questions in the *RACT Guide*

Test 1, page 177, # 54
Test 2, page 318, # 55
Test 3, page 458, # 37
Test 3, page 462, # 49

Test 3, page 464, # 53
Test 4, page 601, # 53
Test 4, page 603, # 58

CHAPTER 6
The Reading Test

"I often carry things to read so that
I will not have to look at the people."

— CHARLES BUKOWSKI

I'm going to give it to you straight: the ACT Reading is one of the most difficult sections to improve in. This is the case because every individual has a different history and relationship with reading.

Some kids love books and have had many years of practice picking out arguments, recognizing rhetorical devices, and building their vocabulary.

Other kids find books boring and have always preferred other activities instead, like firing bottle rockets at the neighbor's cat only to miss and hit the mayor of the city instead, resulting in thousands of dollars of fines and years of humiliation. I speak hypothetically, of course…

While, generally speaking, the life-long readers have an advantage here, there are still some strategies everyone can utilize to improve their reading section score.

Before we begin, you should know…

1. Reading Section Pacing is the Most Difficult of the Test

If there is one section that students run out of time on the most, it is the reading section. And it makes perfect sense when you consider the structure of the test. What is the structure, you ask?

2. Know the Structure of the Reading Test

For most reading tests the structure is as follows:

1 Prose Fiction Passage   (10 questions)

1 Humanities Passage   (10 questions)

1 Social Sciences Passage   (10 questions)

1 Natural Sciences Passage   (10 questions)

This means you have to answer 40 questions in 35 minutes. While this might not seem so bad, this leaves you with eight minutes and 15 seconds to read an entire 800-900 word passage and answer 10 questions about it. Not the easiest thing in the world to do.

So what should we do?

3. Take Practice Tests and Adjust Accordingly

Similar to what we did with the Math test, depending on how fast you read, you might want to consider adjusting your goal of how many questions you try to answer.

If your goal is to score in the mid-20s, and you are naturally a slower reader, it might not make sense to rush through four passages and get more questions incorrect, when you could spend more time and care on just three passages and get more of those questions right.

THE 5 WAYS YOU WILL CONQUER THE *Reading* TEST

1. Come Up With an Answer in Your Head

The Reading test is a fast-paced, stressful section to take.

In the heat of the moment, what most students do is quickly read a question and immediately read the answer choices without thinking about what the answer to the question should be. By doing this they allow the incorrect answer choices to sway them in the wrong direction. This not only creates indecision, which wastes time, but it makes it more likely they will choose an incorrect answer.

The reason why it's so easy to be swayed by the wrong answer choices on the Reading test is most of them include some word or phrase that was in the passage.

So if the passage was discussing the possibility of monkey astronauts traveling to Mars, every answer choice will probably have the word monkey, astronauts, Mars, or any combination of them.

WRONG READING QUESTION PROCESS

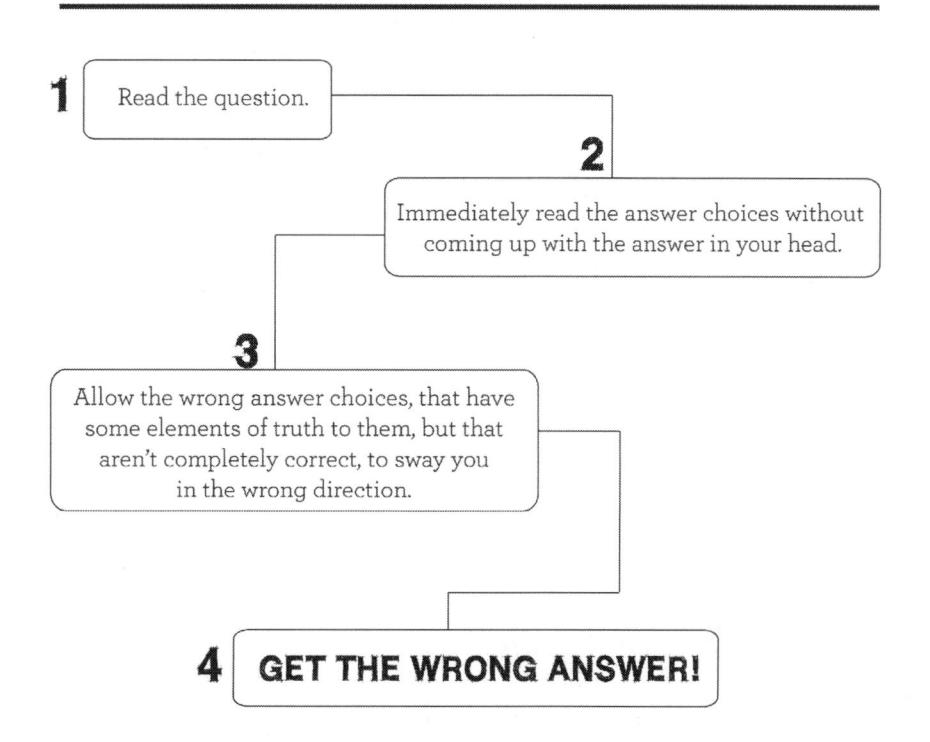

1 Read the question.

2 Immediately read the answer choices without coming up with the answer in your head.

3 Allow the wrong answer choices, that have some elements of truth to them, but that aren't completely correct, to sway you in the wrong direction.

4 GET THE WRONG ANSWER!

Seeing this, the student thinks, "Oh yeah! They did talk about monkey astronauts in Mars!" and circles the answer choice without realizing that while the passage may have been arguing that monkey astronaut missions to Mars should be feasible in this century, the answer they circled was saying the exact opposite.

To answer these questions more efficiently, cover up the answer choices with your hand and read the question. Once and only once you have in your head what you think the answer should be, remove your hand from the answer choices, and compare what you have in your head to what is on the page. Whatever doesn't match with your answer should be crossed out.

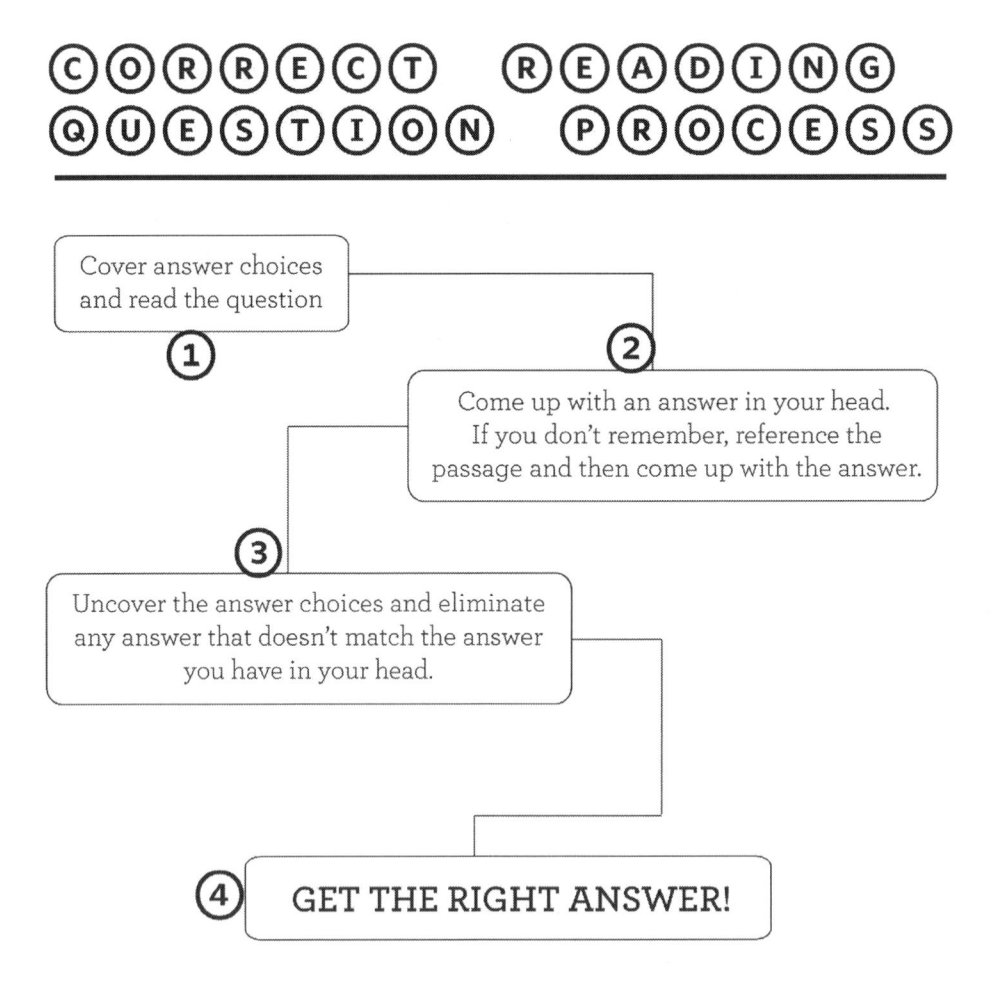

CORRECT READING QUESTION PROCESS

1. Cover answer choices and read the question

2. Come up with an answer in your head. If you don't remember, reference the passage and then come up with the answer.

3. Uncover the answer choices and eliminate any answer that doesn't match the answer you have in your head.

4. GET THE RIGHT ANSWER!

In the case that you really have no clue about what the answer might be, you should go back to the part of the passage that contains relevant information for answering that question and then come up with what the answer should look like.

If worse comes to worst, and you don't even know where to be looking in the passage for the answer, and you're not given a reference to a specific line or paragraph, you can briefly glance at the answer choices to find exactly where in the passage those things are mentioned. This way you can hone in and either eliminate or keep the answer choice. This should be your last resort, however.

This strategy is all about weeding out an inefficient thought process that is perfectly natural for students to take on. But by repeatedly practicing the new one, we can weed out the old and replace it with the new and improved.

Come Up With an Answer in Your Head: *In Summary*

- Almost all Reading test answer choices will have some word or phrase that was mentioned in the passage.
- To more accurately pick the correct answer choice, come up with what you think the answer should be, before going through the answer choices.

2. Get Context

If you stop to think about it, the answers to the questions in the reading section are all right in front of your eyes. So why do so many students get these questions wrong?

Whenever a student is given a line reference question, most will look directly at the lines in question. Not above it, not below it, but exactly at the lines in question. The problem with this is, guess where the information you need to solve the question is. Above and below the line(s) being referenced!

It's cruel, isn't it? That the makers of the ACT do this knowing how students will behave. But hey, if students are going to keep falling for this trick, then why change it?

So when you see a line reference…

- *Read the sentence in which the line reference is contained*
- *Read a sentence or two before*
- *Read a sentence or two after*

This seems really simple, but it's incredibly rare to see students do this on their own. Most students will stare directly at the line reference in question and just think really hard about what the answer might be.

Exercise: *Read the following excerpts and answer the questions that follow, making sure to read a sentence before and a sentence after after each line in question.*

35 *As he spoke he fearlessly patted the head he had so mercilessly pounded, and though Buck's hair involuntarily bristled at touch of the hand, he endured it without protest. When the man brought him water he drank eagerly, and later bolted a generous meal of raw meat, chunk by chunk, from the man's hand.*

40 *He was beaten (he knew that); but he was not broken. He saw, once for all, that he stood no chance against a man with a club. He had learned the lesson, and in all his after life he never forgot it. That club was a revelation. It was his introduction to the reign of primitive law, and he met the introduction halfway. The facts of life took on a fiercer*
45 *aspect; and while he faced that aspect uncowed, he faced it with all the latent cunning of his nature aroused.*

1. What does the author mean by "the lesson" mentioned (line 42)?

15 *But no living man had looted this treasure house, and the dead were dead; wherefore John Thornton and Pete and Hans, with Buck and half a dozen other dogs, faced into the East on an unknown trail to achieve where men and dogs as good as themselves had failed. They sledded seventy miles up the Yukon, swung to the left into the Stewart River, passed the Mayo and the McQuestion, and held on until the*
20 *Stewart itself became a streamlet, threading the upstanding peaks which marked the backbone of the continent."*

2. What is the quest described in "to achieve where men and dogs as good as themselves had failed" (lines 24-27)?

50 I set to and enjoyed a hearty meal. When I had done, I looked for a bell, so that I might let the servants know I had finished; but I could not find one. There are certainly odd deficiencies in the house. This is evident when considering the extraordinary evidences of wealth which are round me. The table service is of gold, and so beautifully wrought that it must be of immense value. The curtains and upholstery of the
60 chairs and sofas and the hangings of my bed are of the costliest and most beautiful fabrics, and must have been of fabulous value when they were made, for they are centuries old, though in excellent order. I saw something like them in Hampton Court, but there they were worn and frayed and moth-eaten. But still in none of the rooms is there a
45 mirror. There is not even a toilet glass on my table, and I had to get the little shaving glass from my bag before I could either shave or brush my hair. I have not yet seen a servant anywhere, or heard a sound near the castle except the howling of wolves.

3. What is meant by the odd deficiencies (line 52)?

Get Context: *In Summary*

When you see a line reference in a question…

- *Read the sentence in which the line reference is contained*
- *Read a sentence or two before*
- *Read a sentence or two after*

Additional **Get Context** Questions in the *RACT Guide*

Test 1, page 185, # 27
Test 1, page 185, # 30
Test 1, page 187, # 34
Test 1, page 187, # 36
Test 2, page 321, # 9
Test 2, page 323, # 16
Test 2, page 325, # 26
Test 2, page 325, # 29
Test 3, page 467, # 7
Test 3, page 469, # 19
Test 3, page 471, # 26

Test 3, page 473, # 35

Test 4, page 607, # 18
Test 4, page 607, # 19
Test 4, page 611, # 33
Test 4, page 611, # 38
Test 5, page 749. # 5
Test 5, page 751, # 13
Test 5, page 751, # 17
Test 5, page 755, # 36
Test 5, page 755, # 39

3. Underline Keywords

This is another strategy all about efficiency. Let's look at a sample test question to see what I mean:

45. *In the context of the passage as a whole, it is most reasonable to infer that the author's mother enjoys which of the following fruits?*

   A. Pears
   B. Bananas
   C. Grapefruit
   D. Cherries

Now, at first glance this question might look fine to us. However, upon closer inspection, we will see there is a lot of fluff in the question that is unnecessary.

The average student rushes through the question and searches the passage for the answer. After searching they go back to the question and re-read it to remind themselves what they are looking for.

By reading the question in its entirety again, they just wasted time reading 23 words that they did not need to. That may not seem like a lot, but if you do this for multiple questions on the reading test, you can lose significant time and significant points.

Let's take another look at the question. This time, I want you to tell me the only three words we need to focus on to answer the question.

> *In the context of the passage as a whole, it is most reasonable to infer that the author's mother enjoys which of the following fruits?*

When you think you have it, move to the next page…

"Author's mother enjoys." That's it.

Underline Keywords: *In Summary*

- The first time you read through the question, underline only the most crucial parts of it.

- This will save you unnecessary time wasting and the lost effort of reading filler words in the question.

4. Check Every Part of the Answer

Many answer choices on Reading test questions have more than one part to them. For example…

Your history teacher catches you texting on on your cell phone during your final exam. What should you do?

A. Apologize to her and then tell her that everyone knows she uses a toupee
B. Apologize and explain you were turning it off to avoid distractions during the test
C. Ignore her and continue to text your BFF
D. Bark like a dog and throw your cell phone at Maggie. No one likes Maggie anyway…

No texting in school…

Every answer choice here has two parts to it, and therefore, you have to make sure that every part is correct. If any part of a question is incorrect, you have to immediately eliminate it.

So, even though answer choice A starts off with apologizing to your teacher, which is relatively good advice, the last part of the answer will most likely make the situation end badly for you.

Because they feel pressed for time, many students will circle an answer at the first sign of having one correct part to it. The makers of the ACT know this and for this reason, purposely create answer choices that are partly (but not fully) true.

Don't fall into this trap: Check every part of every answer choice before either eliminating or choosing it.

Check Every Part of the Answer: *In Summary*

- Many answers have elements of truth to them, but are not completely true

- You need to check and make sure that every part of the answer choice matches before choosing it

Additional **Check Every Part…** Questions in the *RACT Guide*

Test 1, page 181, # 2
Test 1, page 183, # 12
Test 1, page 183, # 13
Test 2, page 321, # 5
Test 2, page 321, # 6
Test 2, page 322, # 11

Test 2, page 323, # 19
Test 2, page 327, # 33
Test 3, page 467, # 2
Test 4, page 605, # 6
Test 4, page 609 # 24

5. Don't Overdo Note-Taking and Underlining

Some students get carried away while going through the reading passages, and underline every other word and take notes every other line. By doing so, however, they miss sight of the fact that what's most important on the Reading section is to *understand* the passages. Because we are crunched for time here, spending too much of it writing down or underlining non-essential information will hurt rather than help you.

There are the right and wrong ways to take notes on the reading passages:

The wrong way to take notes…

History has taught us that passing mandates with the intention of changing human behavior does not work. The prohibition era in the United States, the period from 1920 to 1933 in which the production, importation, and transportation of alcohol were banned, is a such a lesson from history. Although alcohol was criminalized during this time period, people still found ways to consume it in hidden make-shift bars called speakeasies, and suppliers were able to feed the demand by smuggling alcohol from Canada or by distilling it themselves. Similarly, if junk food in high school vending machines were banned, it would only motivate students to find other ways to consume junk food such as bringing unhealthy snacks from home or getting fast food after school ends.

Annotations: "Alcohol was illegal 1920-1933", "EWW!"

The right way to take notes...

~~History has taught us that passing mandates with the intention of changing human behavior does not work.~~ The prohibition era in the United States, the period from 1920 to 1933 in which the production, importation, and transportation of alcohol were banned, is a such a lesson from history. Although alcohol was criminalized during this time period, people still found ways to consume it in hidden make-shift bars called speakeasies, and suppliers were able to feed the demand by smuggling alcohol from Canada or by distilling it themselves. Similarly, <u>if junk food in high school vending machines were banned, it would only motivate students to find other ways to consume junk food</u> such as bringing unhealthy snacks from home or getting fast food after school ends.

[margin note: prohibition]

When it comes to marking-up passages, less is more!

Later, when you go back to the passage to answer the questions, you will easily see the essential information of this paragraph: that the author believes banning junk food in high school wouldn't help students make better nutritional choices, and that he uses prohibition as an example.

Write notes and underline the bare minimum necessary to help you *understand* the passage better when you need to reference it later.

Don't Overdo Note-Taking and Underlining: *In Summary*

- spending too much time writing down or underlining non-essential information will hurt rather than help you

- only underline and write notes the least amount necessary to be able to quickly reference the passage when you're answering questions

6. ACT Test Writers are Politically Correct

Before I go into a diatribe about how political correctness undermines freedom of speech in the United States today, let's…just…not.

But political correctness is indeed important for the ACT because the test writers themselves seem to love it, and we can use this to our advantage.

On the Reading section, whenever you see an answer choice that's not P.C., you can always cross it out. What exactly does a non-PC answer choice look like? Any answer choice that's mean, brash, offensive, discriminatory, or makes generalizations or sweeping claims you should consider a no-go.

So, if you see an answer choice about bringing back slavery, cross it out.

If an answer choice suggests that all Americans are uneducated, cross it out.

Another way to think about it is this: if an answer choice seems like it could inspire someone to make a 20-minute-long YouTube rant about how offended they are by it, cross it out.

ACT Test Writers are Politically Correct: *In Summary*

- The ACT loves to be politically correct. Any answer choice that's remotely offensive or makes broad generalizations can be crossed out.

Additional **ACT Test Writers are P.C.** Questions in the *RACT Guide*

Test 1, page 182, # 11
Test 1, page 183, # 20
Test 1, page 185, # 27
Test 2, page 322, # 11
Test 3, page 471, # 25
Test 5, page 755, # 33

CHAPTER 7
The Science Test

"Two things are infinite: the universe and human stupidity; and I'm not so sure about the former."

— Albert Einstein

I want you to imagine something for me.

Imagine you are forced to watch a movie in a language that you don't understand. Not only do you not speak the language, but throughout this three-hour-long movie, you're asked to find the exact moment when a lady with purple hair runs across the screen.

What do this ridiculous hypothetical scenario and the ACT Science section have in common? During both, you have to endure completely confusing circumstances while staying hyper-focused.

In this section you'll see strange symbols, convoluted charts, and words that look like they belong to an alien language. You will feel confused, but that's OK. In fact, the passages in this section are so obscure and technical that I would wager most PhD biologists, chemists, engineers, and physicists wouldn't comprehend 95 percent of them!

Moral of the story: don't let the scientific jargon and strange diagrams freak you out. As you're about to see, there are a couple of things that when combined with perseverance and focus will allow any student can do to improve their score on the Science section.

Before we begin, you should know...

1. **For the majority of questions, you do not need to know anything about science.**

   Woo hoo! This means you can succeed on the science test no matter what science class you're currently in. You can breathe easily.

2. **However, a few questions do require knowledge of basic scientific concepts.**

   With the above point being said, there may be a question or two in this section that you do in fact need previous scientific knowledge to answer.

   Basic things such as reading a chemical equation, knowing that metal conducts heat better than wood, recognizing the difference between a dominant and a recessive allele, and knowing what a limiting reactant is are all topics they could ask about here.

   In any regard, it's not worth it to worry about these. They are usually less than two or three questions that presuppose this information, and it's usually basic concepts. Your time will be better spent going over practice science tests than studying random scientific concepts.

3. **Get used to your brain being fried**

   I always thought it was so cruel that they put the Science section at the very end. You've just used all this brainpower finishing three difficult sections and now you have to deal with confusing scientific charts and jargon? Not fair by a long shot.

   However, this is why it's key to take as many full practice tests as possible, as you near your test date, to experience and adjust to the mental fatigue you'll feel while taking the Science section. The more you do practice, the more comfortable you will become with taking this tricky section.

THE 5 WAYS YOU WILL Conquer THE SCIENCE TEST

1. The Three Types of Science Section Passages

There are always only three types of passages you will see in this section, and it's important to familiarize yourself with each of them.

A. **Data Representation Passages** - These are passages filled with charts, graphs, tables, and other visual data representations. The Science section has three of these passages.

B. **Research Summaries Passages** - Descriptions of several related experiments. They also have diagrams and tables quite similar to data representations. The Science section has three of these passages.

C. **Conflicting Viewpoints Passages** - Two scientists have two different theories. It's your job to be able to summarize those theories and compare and contrast them with one another. These passages are markedly different from the other two in that it feels more like a passage you would see in the Reading section. The Science section has only one of these passages.

Exercise: *Go through each passage of each Science test in the RACT Guide and label each passage as DR, RS, or CV..*

2. Don't Read (For the Most Part…)

Reading is obviously necessary for the reading section. Reading is important for the english section. But, for the most part, reading is not important for the Science section.

Data Representation and Research Summaries
Little reading required

For Data Representation and Research Summaries passages, you usually can answer all of the questions without ever reading the paragraph text. If you look carefully, you'll notice that most of the text is just repeating what is already shown in the table or chart. In most cases, the most efficient way to answer the questions for these passages is by solely using the data in the graphs, charts, and tables.

Now, here and there there may be a tidbit of information in the text important for defining a variable or for making sense of the data. In general though, for DR and RS passages, we can breeze right on by most information.

Conflicting Viewpoints:
the reading passage turned science passage

The only passage in which we actually do need to read the paragraph text is the Conflicting Viewpoints passage. Reading is crucial here because we need to fully understand each scientist's argument and contrast and compare them before we can answer the questions. As I mentioned before, this passage is really a reading passage with an identity crisis.

Exercise: *Practice seeing just how many Science section questions you can answer without reading any text from the passages. You might just surprise yourself!*

3. Get Acquainted

How many tables are there?
How many graphs are there?
What are they measuring?
What are your axes?

Getting a sense of what you're about to jump into will help you more efficiently answer these questions. As we've seen, for Data Representation and Research Summaries passages, about 90 percent of the questions are going to come from the graphs, tables, and figures themselves –again– NOT from the text.

So every time you flip the page and begin the next science passage, take a quick glance at the data and the graphs before jumping into the questions. It will help give you an edge on the section.

4. It's All About Relationships

I'll say it again: you don't need to know much about science to do well on the Science section. For the Data Representation and Research Summary passages, you do not actually need to understand what's going on. You just need to be able to see patterns, trends, and relationships between two variables.

So, in other words, as one variable changes how does another change? As you increase one variable, the other variable could increase, decrease, increase and then decrease, or stay the same.

Check out the relationships between variables in the following graphs:

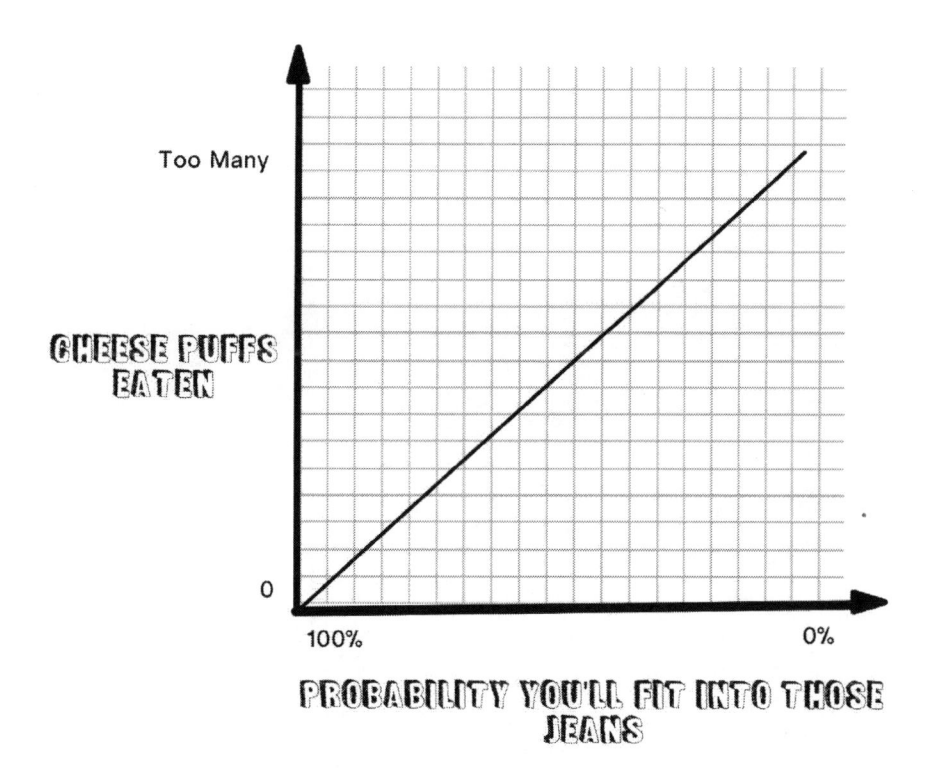

Trend: As the number of cheese puffs eaten increses the probability you'll fit into those jeans decreases.

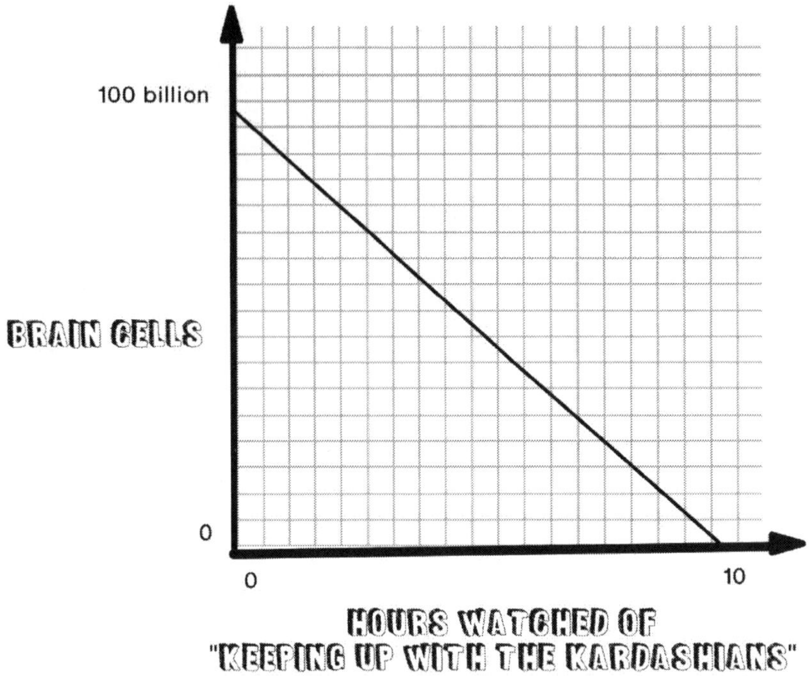
100 billion
BRAIN CELLS
0
0
10
HOURS WATCHED OF
"KEEPING UP WITH THE KARDASHIANS"

Trend: As the hours watched of "Keeping Up With the Kardashians" increases, the number of brain cells decreases.

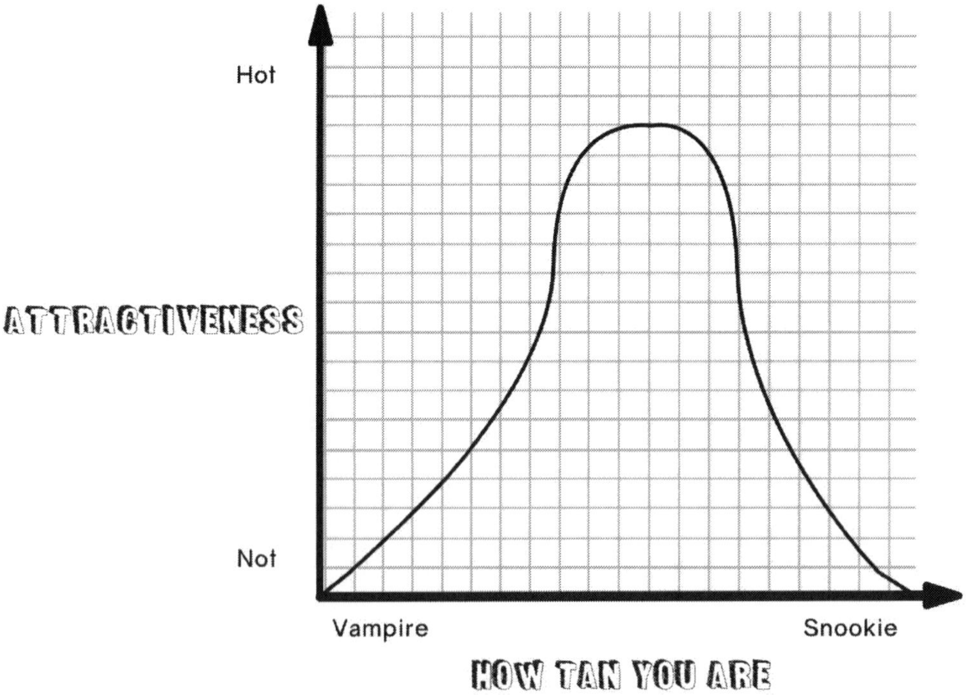
Hot
ATTRACTIVENESS
Not
Vampire
Snookie
HOW TAN YOU ARE

Trend: As tan-ness increases, attractiveness increases and then decreases.

It's All About Relationships: *In Summary*

- In Data Representation and Research Summaries passages, you need to understand very little about the actual experiment.

- Most questions in these passages gauge a superficial understanding of relationships and trends between variables in the charts, tables, and figures.

5. The Three Types of Variables

A **variable** is any factor, trait, or condition that can be measured: One variable could be bodyweight, another variable could be age, and another distance travelled. Simply put, a variable is anything that can be measured when performing an experiment.

There are three types of variables:

Independent Variables
Dependent Variables
Controlled Variables

To better explain the differences between these three, we will be using a brilliant experiment that I conducted for my eighth grade science fair, in which I watered plants using water and various other liquids (soda, vinegar, Gatorade, and chocolate milk) in order to see if there would be an effect on plant height. Fascinating, right?

1. **Independent variables** are what the scientist directly changes in the experiment.

In my experiment, my independent variable was the liquid that I gave to each plant. This changed for each plant, as some received water and others received vinegar, soda, Gatorade or chocolate milk.

2. **Dependent variables** are what changes in response to changing the independent variable.

The dependent variable in my experiment was plant height. As the liquid for each plant changed, the plant height changed as a result.

3. **Controlled variables** are those that are kept constant in order to confidently say that a change in what we're measuring is due only to the change in our independent variable.

In my experiment, to make sure that the difference in plant height was only due to the change in the liquid I gave them, I kept the temperature in the room, the position of the plant, and the time of day I watered the plants constant throughout the course of the experiment.

Exercise: *List the independent, dependent, and controlled variables in the following experimental scenarios.*

1. Janet decides she wants to see if the food she feeds her twin brothers will affect their weight. She decides to feed one of the twins nothing but carrots. To the other twin she feeds nothing but pepperoni pizza. She feeds them the same amount of calories of each food and at the same time each day.

2. Dave is tired of his son getting bad grades in his classes so he decides to try a new approach. To try and improve his sons grades, Dave buys his son a bowl of ice cream every time he gets an A on an assignment. He makes sure to buy him the same size and flavor of ice cream every time.

3. Gina gets the sniffles a lot and decides to take a vitamin-C supplement to try and decrease the number of days she spends with the sniffles. She takes the same amount of the supplement at the same time each day.

The Three Types of Variables: *In Summary...*

VARIABLE	INDEPENDENT	DEPENDENT	CONTROLLED
DEFINITION	what the experimenter directly changes in the experiment	what changes in response to the changing independent variable	things that are kept constant to make sure the change to the ind. variable is the real reason for change in the dep. variable
EXAMPLE FROM MY EXPERIMENT	water, vinegar, soda, gatorade, chocolate milk	height of each plant	amount of liquid watered, room temperature, position of the plant, time of day watered

CHAPTER 8
The Essay

"Writing in English is like throwing mud at a wall."

– Joseph Conrad

Many students make the ACT essay out to be scarier than it actually is. Before we go into the details of exactly how you're going to nail this section, here's some important background information about the essay that you might not have known.

The Essay is Not Optional (if you want to be a competitive applicant)

You are given an option to take the test with or without the essay section. While it might be tempting to take the easy way out and opt not to write it, I always recommend to my students to take the essay. As long as you take a couple of principles in mind and write a decent essay, it will make you a more competitive applicant in the eyes of college admissions offices. And isn't that the whole point of all this anyway?

The Essay is the Last Section and the Least Important

The essay comes after the English, Math, Reading, and Science sections, and by that time you will have used a lot of brain power. The fact that the essay is the final hurdle of the race is the thing that, in my opinion, makes the it seem like one of the toughest sections on the test.

Regardless, don't worry too much about it. The essay is by far the least important section in the whole test. How well you do on the essay does not affect your subject area scores or your composite score. The only difference when you take the ACT with the essay is you that you will receive a **Writing sub-score** which is used to create a separate **Combined English/Writing score.** Not that important.

Practice Makes Perfect

You should take as many timed 40-minute ACT essays as you need to until you feel confident about the essay section. For every student this number will be different: for some it will be two; for others it might be 8. Only you can know how many you will need under your belt until you feel ready.

THE 6 SIMPLE WAYS YOU WILL Conquer THE *Essay*

!! READ ME !!

Since this book was published, the ACT has decided to change their essay section. All ACT writing tests after September of 2015 will have a new essay format, which will change the approach you must take to answer the prompt.

Until we are able to research and better understand how to prepare for the new essay, **please disregard tip number 2 below, which included past essay prompts and suggestions for how to write your body paragraphs**. The rest of the tips, however, are still relevant and valuable to constructing your essay.

Thank you for being patient in this transition while we adapt to these unforeseen changes.

1. **Forget about the Five-Paragraph Essay**

   For decades upon decades, English teachers across the nation have led young and impressionable students to believe that the best short essay length was five paragraphs.

   But you have to remember: this isn't school. This is the ACT. You only have 40 minutes to brainstorm, write, and proofread a stellar essay. And given this time constraint, because quality is more important than quantity, you will most likely be better off writing a four-paragraph essay with an introduction, two body paragraphs, and a conclusion.

   Of course, if you are very confident about your ability as a writer, and feel that the fifth paragraph will add to the quality of your essay, then and only then should you write that extra body paragraph.

2. ~~**All Essay Prompts are Virtually the Same**~~

   Something I realized after completing practice test after practice test was that almost all essay prompts on the ACT revolved around the same topic: *should the government, educators, etc. make educational reforms that will impact high-school students.* Yes or no?

   Here are some examples of essay prompts that have appeared on actual tests:

   - *Should teenagers be required to maintain a "C" average in school to receive a driver's license?*

   - *Should high schools require students to complete a certain number of hours of community service?*

   - *Should high schools create separate classes for male and female students?*

   - *Should television channels be required to dedicate at least 20 percent of programming to educational shows?*

   - *Should students be allowed to choose the books he or she reads for English class?*

Now that we know what kind of question we'll be answering, we can prepare for it better.

In the likely case that your essay prompt regards a mandate, I recommend that you always oppose the mandate and structure your essay in the following way.

How to Write Your Body Paragraphs

Body Paragraph 1: Mandates are ineffective at changing human behavior.

Humans will act however they want to, regardless of the laws in place. If laws were effective at shaping human behavior, why then, in a society where murder, theft, and driving under the influence are all illegal, do we still experience these things?

Historical example: **The Prohibition era in the U.S.**

The Prohibition era in the United States was a period from 1920 to 1933 in which the production, importation, and transportation of alcohol were banned. Although alcohol was criminalized during this time period, people still found ways to consume it in hidden make-shift bars called speakeasies, and suppliers were able to feed the demand by smuggling alcohol from Canada or by distilling it themselves.

Body Paragraph 2: The passage of reforms like this could lead a free society down a treacherous path leading to authoritarianism.

Giving a government the ability to pass mandates so long as they are justified as being for the good of the people leaves us vulnerable to a legislature passing any law, taking any action, no matter how oppressive they might be.

Quote: *"Most of the evil in this world is done by people with good intentions.*
         - T.S. Eliot

Historical Example: Cambodian genocide by the Khmer Rouge and Pol Pot

Between 1975 and 1979, one quarter of Cambodia's population was killed by Pol Pot and the Khmer Rouge, a group of well educated students who had the intention of creating a new rural, classless society. In their attempt to socially engineer a classless peasant society, they took particular aim at intellectuals, city residents, ethnic Vietnamese, civil servants and religious leaders, exterminating two million people by the end of 1979.

Although it's very likely the essay will deal with a mandate, keep in mind that there's a small chance it will not be. That's OK. In this case, just make sure you closely follow the rest of the essay tips and you will be fine.

Practice applying this format to several ACT practice prompts, and you will be much better equipped to tackle whatever essay questions gets thrown your way on test day.

3. The Introduction is the Most Important Paragraph

First impressions are important. It's a fact of life.

It's why you wouldn't show up to a first date sporting pajamas and bad breath. It's also why you want to be very careful about making sure your introduction is as strong as possible.

ACT essay graders spend only two to three minutes looking over your essay, and chances are that within just the first 30 seconds of reading, they've already made some judgement about how good your essay is and what kind of score it deserves.

Have a Strong Thesis Statement

Make sure your stance on the topic is clear and isn't on the fence. You must argue one way or the other. No flip-flopping!
Also, make sure your thesis statement perfectly encapsulates the argument you

make in your body paragraphs.

Because mandates are ineffective at shaping human behavior and enacting this law would lead our society closer to authoritarianism, laws banning junk food in high school vending machines should not be adopted.

4. **Make Sure Your Essay Has a Strong Core**

   To make sure your essay has clarity and is relevant to the prompt, you must ensure it has a strong foundation, or core.

   What do I mean by "core"?

   Your core is your thesis statement, your paragraph 1 topic sentence and your paragraph 2 topic sentence.

   If a complete stranger were to read just these three sentences she should be able to understand the main argument of the essay just as well as someone who read it in its entirety.

   This is absolutely essential to make sure your essay is as well-organized and as tight as it can be.

5. **Refute the Counterargument**

   A good essay gets a score of 8. A superior essay gets a score of 12. How can we make our essays superior?

   Why, by acknowledging the counterargument to your stance, of course!

   Being able to put yourself in the position of someone who thinks differently than you do is a sign of high-order thinking, and ACT graders love to see this.

   So if your prompt asks, "*Should high schools ban the sale of unhealthy snacks in vending machines?*" and your stance is that they should not, you could acknowledge, and subsequently refute the counterargument in the following way:

While some may believe that limiting the availability of junk food in high school vending machines will encourage students to choose healthier options and lead healthier lifestyles, in reality, it will only motivate students to find other ways to consume junk food such as bringing unhealthy snacks from home, or getting fast food after school ends.

A very small percentage of students do this in their essay. By doing this you will show the essay grader that you are thinking critically about both sides of the argument.

6. Be Different, Not Predictable.

An essay score of 6 is average, the norm, what everyone else is doing. You don't want to be average. You want to be different. Different is good. Different can get us closer to that 12. So, how can you be different?

Don't repeat the prompt verbatim

If the essay prompt is "*Should high schools ban the sale of unhealthy snacks in vending machines?*" you can be certain that 99 percent of students are going to begin their introductions with, "*I believe high schools should not ban the sale of unhealthy snacks in vending machines because blah, blah, blah.*"

Instead, make an impression and break the mold. Be different.

"*Colored lockers line the halls of high school hallways. On the way to class, students stop at vending machines to purchase their favorite snack. While such a scene is commonplace today, certain lawmakers are attempting to pass legislation to change this.*"

Use examples, but not cliché examples

I highly recommend you research further and use the examples I've given you of the U.S. Prohibition era as well as the Cambodian genocide. These examples will help set you apart from the pack.

However, feel free to use examples of your own. Just make sure you're not using examples that every other student is going to use.

Historical figures like Abraham Lincoln, Mahatma Gandhi, and FDR; historical events like World War II or the Great Depression. Books such as *The Great Gatsby*, *The Catcher in the Rye*, or *The Scarlett Letter*: these are the examples that most students will use in their essays. **Avoid using these examples at all costs.**

Use Varied Sentence Structure

I want to talk about something very important. I want to show you how boring it is to read writing that uses the same sentence structure over and over. I know that you might already be aware of this in your own writing. I also know that you might not already be aware of it. I just truly want you to know that by varying the structure of sentences, utilizing questions instead of just statements, and trying to convey the same idea in different ways you will improve the essay grader's experience of your essay.

Did I make my point?

Now that you've read all of the tips for constructing a superior essay, let's put it into practice.

An Exceptional Essay Embodying our Six Principles

Prompt: **Should high schools prohibit the sale of junk food in vending machines?**

No one can deny: obesity is a pervasive problem in the United States today. It is estimated that over 15 percent of American children and adolescents are obese, while the figure for adults is twice as great. In order to combat this epidemic, several lawmakers have proposed the passage of legislation that would ban the sale of junk food in high-school vending machines. With restricted access to nutritionally poor snacks, they argue, students would be incentivized to choose healthier alternatives. However, because mandates are ineffective at shaping human behavior and enacting this law would lead our society closer to authoritarianism, laws banning junk food in high-school vending machines should not be adopted.

History has taught us that passing mandates with the intention of changing human behavior does not work. The Prohibition era in the United States, the period from 1920 to 1933 in which the production, importation, and transportation of alcohol were banned, is one such lesson from history. Although alcohol was criminalized during this time period, people still found ways to consume it in hidden make-shift bars called speakeasies, and suppliers were able to feed the demand by smuggling alcohol from Canada or by distilling it themselves. Similarly, if junk food in high school vending machines were banned, it would only motivate students to find other ways to consume junk food, such as bringing unhealthy snacks from home or getting fast food after school ends.

Nobel Prize-winning poet T.S. Eliot once said, *"Most of the evil in this world is done by people with good intentions."* The past clearly shows us the danger of imposing laws in a society with the intention of helping individuals for their own sake. Between 1975 and 1979, one quarter of Cambodia's population was killed by Pol Pot and the Khmer Rouge, a group of well educated students who had the intention of creating a new rural, classless society. In taking action toward what they believed would benefit their country, the Khmer Rouge exterminated 2 million people in only four years. All of this destruction was justified in the name of the greater good. If our society begins to pass legislation solely justified by good intentions even though it infringes on our freedom of choice, such as limiting options in vending machines, we may fall into the trap of authoritarianism.

Noble intentions are necessary for a society to thrive. However, we must be careful not to justify the means with the end. Attempting to force individuals to change is as authoritarian as it is ineffective. If we are aiming to change unhealthy dietary choices, a better solution might be to educate students of all ages about the dangers of leading a nutritionally-poor lifestyle; This education would not only provide individuals with information to help them change their habits, but also preserve their freedom of choice.

The Essay: *In Summary...*

- Forget about the five-paragraph essay. Four paragraphs is your best bet for a quality 30-minute essay (intro, 2 bodies, and conclusion)

- The majority of ACT essay prompts are the same: do you believe a mandate should be enforced in public schools across the U.S.?

    * *When faced with this prompt it's easiest to always oppose the mandate using the structure discussed above**

- First impressions are important even on the ACT. Make sure your intro paragraph is tight and that your thesis statement includes your stance and the arguments you will use to defend that stance. It's the most important paragraph.

- Organization is crucial. A reader should be able to understand the argument of your entire essay from three sentences only: the thesis statement, topic sentence 1, and topic sentence 2.

- Refuting the counterargument and, in general, not being cliché can help your essay avoid the label of average and help it stand out from the rest.

At this point, you have reviewed all the strategies and all of the concepts for every section of the ACT. English, Math, Reading, Science, and the Essay… you've done it all!

I'm sure you'll agree it's been quite a ride. It's true what they say: "Time flies when you're having fun."

Now that you have prepped with all these concepts and strategies, how can we finish strongly in order to ensure we do our best on test day?

CHAPTER 9
The Week of the Test

"If you try to do your best, there is no failure"
-MIKE FARRELL

If you've read the book up until this point, followed all the instruction, and done all the exercises, you will be in excellent shape for the test.

Soon, the time will come when you're only a week away from taking one of the single most important tests of your academic career. And by no means will it be an easy feat; you will have to be on your A-game for four hours straight. In order to finish as strongly as you started, follow these tips.

Sleep

Because your circadian rhythms take at least three days to normalize and be most efficient, the week of the test, make sure you waking up every morning at the time you'll wake up on test day. Then, calculate at what time you'll need to go to bed every night to get your seven to eight hours of sleep, whichever amount your body needs to operate most efficiently.

Make sure you show up early for your test: take into account traffic and unexpected events. You might decide to wake up at 6:30 AM. In order to get 8 hours of sleep, you'll want to go to bed at 10:30 PM.

Food

As usual, make sure to keep your diet clean and healthy the week of the test by abiding by the general food rules in chapter 4. There are a couple food considerations we need to take into account right before the test.

Dinner the Night Before the Test: *Keep It Simple*

The night before, make sure you eat a nutrient-rich dinner no less than 2 hours before bedtime to give your body enough time to digest the food. Otherwise, the digestion will pull away the energy your brain needs to give you a good night's rest.

Breakfast: *No Pop-Tarts*

The morning of the test, it's important you have a breakfast hearty enough to keep you fueled throughout the test but not so heavy that it gives you a food baby that leaves you feeling lethargic. So a ham, steak, egg, and pancake buffet is perhaps not the best option for breakfast.

Sugary cereals, pancakes, pop-tarts, fruit juice and fruit cocktails, and energy drinks will all initially give you a burst of energy and then let you crash less than halfway into the test. More appropriate for test-day breakfast are hardboiled eggs with toast, steel cut oatmeal (not the sugary, packaged kind) with fresh fruit, multigrain cereal with almond milk, or a chocolate protein shake with a banana.

Not exactly the ideal breakfast for test day.

I always recommend that students keep their liquid intake to only H_2O, but if you absolutely must have your coffee, go ahead and have it. But don't overdo it, or you'll find yourself jittery and wanting to go to the bathroom after every section.

During the Test: *Snack Time*

After the Math test you'll be given a short 10-minute break. It's a great opportunity to refuel your mind and body with a snack. Granola bars, celery and peanut butter, apples, oranges, or even a hard-boiled egg will give you a boost to help you finish the last three sections with energy and focus.

Relax the Day Before the Test

You've spent the last several weeks working hard, preparing for the ACT. The day before the test must be reserved for relaxing and unwinding before your performance.

Any studying now will hurt you instead of helping. You have to be at peace with the idea that there's only so much you can do.

The day before the test…

- Don't do any studying.
- Don't stress or obsess.
- Go out with your friends or family to keep your mind occupied.
- Do some exercise if you can.
- Celebrate your preparation! You've worked hard!

CONCLUSION
The Challenges Never Stop

"Being challenged in life is inevitable, being defeated is optional."

— Roger Crawford

Now that you've successfully prepared for the ACT, I'm sure you're wondering: "What's next? What do I do now? When will life finally stop challenging and inconveniencing me?"

The truth is that the challenges never stop.

Once you finish ACT prep, the challenge becomes completing college applications. Once you get into college, the challenge changes to maintaining your GPA and applying for scholarships. Once you graduate college, the challenge becomes finding a career you're fulfilled in. Once you find that career, the challenge turns into applying for the promotion you want.

Rinse and repeat *indefinitely*.

There's a lot of change and challenge in life, but by taking the initiative to buy this book and work through it, you've proved to yourself that you are capable of rising to meet those challenges.

Also, don't forget to continue implementing the fundamentals in this book (psychology, sleep, and nutrition) after the test has ended. They will help you deal with each challenge on your journey a little easier.

Congratulations on conquering the ACT. I knew you could do it.

"Mentoring is a brain to pick, an ear to listen, and a push in the right direction."

—John C. Crosby

- *Are you a motivated student who would like to take your test scores to the next level?*
- *Did you enjoy the book, but have more questions?*
- *Are you interested in the added benefit of personalized instruction?*

If you answered "yes" to the above questions, I would love to extend to you a personal invitation to work with me one-on-one. Not only can I help you with test prep, but I can also provide guidance with essay consulting and admissions interview prep.

I've coached students into the some of the most prestigious universities in the world and worked with clients from all around the globe.

Because student demand is high, I may only have the opportunity to work with a limited number of student requests. To see if you would be a good fit for personalized instruction with me, fill out a short tutoring application at www.testpreplive.com.

I look forward to meeting you soon!

Andre Kiss

Author, Speaker, and Founder of TestPrepLive.Com

ENJOYED THE BOOK?

WANT TO HELP ANOTHER STUDENT?

Give it a 5-star review

★★★★★

on…

the website where you bought this book

(while we both know which one I'm referring to, we can't mention its name for legal reasons…)

The more reviews the book has, the easier it will be for students who need ACT help to find this resource.

By taking a minute of your time you could make a world of difference in a student's life!

I Used to Hate the ACT, too. - Andre Kiss, *founder of* testpreplive.com

Answers to English Practice Problems

Subject-verb Agreement

1. S: Emily   V: decides (NOT "decide")
2. S: Skipping school   V: is
3. S: Litter   V: was (NOT "were")

Semi-colon Test

1. Incorrect (S.C. should be a comma)
2. No error
3. No error

Tense

1. "razed", NOT "raze"
2. "love", NOT "loved"
3. "had finished", NOT "finished"

Parallel Structure

1. planned (NOT "also plans")
2. delivers (NOT "will deliver")
3. No error

Who Loves Commas?

1. The house was around the corner from the movie theater.
2. She likes to drink coffee, unlike Jamie.
3. Jamie and his brother decided to take the day off from work.
4. Last summer, I visited North Carolina and New York.

Avoid the Passive Voice at All Costs

1. The active voice places emphasis on the doer of the action. The passive voice places the emphasis on the object of the action. The ACT prefers the passive voice.

2.a) He has never been to the Bahamas because he is always too busy working.

   b) No error.

   c) Charlie, promoted to the rank of Sergeant, was elated.

3. "Being", "having been", and having -ed, -en (eaten, watched, talked.)

Its, it's and its'

1. it's
2. its
3. its
4. it's

Answers to Math Practice Problems

Never Work in Fractions

1. 4%
2. .375 cups of flour
3. ~ 11 feet and 2 inches

The Distance Formula

1. $5\sqrt{2}$
2. $4\sqrt{2}$
3. 5 miles

Average

1. 88.6
2. 192 cm
3. $ 21.667

Combinations

1. 900,000
2. 120
3. 36

Get Concrete

1. E
2. C
3. B

Percents

1. 285%
2. $58,406
3. 40.5%

Plug n' Chug

1. F= -24
2. k = 4000
3. T= 1.42

Slope

1. y_2-y_1/x_2-x_1

2. a) $-5/7$
   b) $16/11$
   c) $4/15$

3. a) $7/5$
   b) $-11/16$
   c) $-15/4$

Become a master of y=mx+b

1. a) y=-5x+16
   b) -5 and $1/5$
   c) 16

2. a) y=2x+$3/2$
   b) 2 and $-1/2$
   c) $3/2$

3. a) y=$\frac{1}{8}$x-4
   b) $\frac{1}{8}$ and -8
   c) -4

Exponents

1. 2
2. 1
3. ½
4. 3
5. 5
6. 1

Log

1. log (xy)²
2a. x=44
2b. x=1

Functions

1. -5
2. 4
3. f(x)+3 would shift the graph up 3 units, while f(x-3) would shift the graph right 3 units.

Angles and Angle-Algebra

1. y = 18
2. 21.88
3. 202.5

Triangle

1. 20
2. 4<x<18
3. 18π

Circle

1. 300
2. 80 high heels.
3. 30.1 feet.

Circle Equation

1. $(x-6)^2+(y+10) = 16$
2. $(x+4)^2+(y+5) = 36$
3. $(x-3)^2+(y+5) = 25$

SOH-CAH-TOA

1. a) secant b) cotangent c) cosecant
2. 16/20
3. 28.6 feet

Other Trig Stuff

1. 3/5
2. 4π
3. 0.667 π
4. 1.5 π

Answers to Reading Test Practice Problems

Get Context

1. He never stood a chance against a man with a club.

2. Looting the treasure house.

3. In the house there were things of immense value, but not even a bell or a mirror.

Answers to Science Test Practice Problems

Three types of variables

1. independent variable: food given (pizza and carrots)
   dependent variable: the weight of the twins
   controlled variables: number of calories of each food

2. independent variable: bowl of ice cream
   dependent variable: grades of Dave's son
   controlled variable: size and flavor of ice cream

3. independent variable: vitamin C supplement
   dependent variable: days spent with sniffles
   controlled variable: amount of supplement and time it was taken each day

Made in the USA
Lexington, KY
02 October 2017